A DEATH IN THE FAMILY

The death of someone close is one of the hardest of life's experiences. Family and friends are faced with a bewildering series of decisions and arrangements, often for the first time. This book is designed to help with all these practical matters, explaining them and making them as easy as possible.

But the emotional and spiritual side is even more important than the practical questions. Jean Richardson writes out of her own experience as a widow left to bring up a family. She also draws on the experience of others as she guides the reader through the various stages of grief. Her book, written from the perspective of Christian belief, is thoughtful and reassuring, full of practical help and real hope for the future.

Jean Richardson's husband died suddenly and unexpectedly in 1965. Her three sons were then aged eight, thirteen and sixteen. Not wanting to take a full-time job while they were still at school, she became a freelance writer. She has written and spoken widely on the subjects of bereavement and one-parent families, and has become well-known as a regular broadcaster.

A Death in the Family

JEAN RICHARDSON

A LION GUIDE

Tring · Belleville · Sydney

Text copyright © 1979 Jean Richardson
This illustrated edition © 1985 Lion Publishing

Published by
Lion Publishing Corporation
10885 Textile Road, Belleville, Michigan 48111, USA
ISBN 0 85648 815 1

First edition 1979
Second edition 1982
This edition 1985

Acknowledgments
Edited for US edition by Evelyn Bence
Illustrations by Ron Ferns and Kathy Wyatt
Cover Photograph by Picture Bank Photo Library Ltd

Printed and bound in Great Britain by
Cox and Wyman Ltd, Reading

CONTENTS

INTRODUCTION   7

THE FIRST FEW DAYS   9

UNDERSTANDING DEATH   17

REALIZATION   20

COPING WITH GRIEF   29

MOURNING   41

WHAT WILL IT MEAN?   46

EMOTIONAL PROBLEMS   59

WHERE TO LIVE—AND HOW   65

EARNING A LIVING   70

THE BEREAVED CHILD   76

THE ONE-PARENT FAMILY   83

HOW CAN OTHERS HELP?   86

PREPARING FOR BEREAVEMENT   92

INTRODUCTION

Death has suddenly become personal; it has hit where it hurts most, and you find you have to live the rest of your life without someone you loved.

This book has been written to help with the practical questions, emotional problems, spiritual matters—how to arrange a funeral, deal with a will, understand your irritability, let a room, find a job, and everything in between. There are also sections on grief and mourning to help you understand why you feel as you do, and what you can do to help yourself and those around you through this difficult time.

SECURITY

Bereavement snatches away our most basic human security. Our world crumbles, and we fall to our knees. The way in which we handle a crisis such as this depends much on our attitudes and beliefs. Personally, as a Christian, I could not have survived being widowed without the presence and strength of God, and prayers of fellow Christians and the support of friends.

MAKE OR BREAK

An experience of such depth and magnitude as the death of a member of our family can either make or break us; it can destroy us, or it can mark a growing-point which leads to a new beginning. Death is part of life and it cannot be avoided; some time or other in life everyone comes face to face with it. It is always unexpected, always unwelcome and always causes pain.

With the pain come all sorts of other symptoms, and they usually follow a pattern—almost like an illness. As with an illness, with care and help, we recover, but while the illness lasts we see no end to it. Such is bereavement.

No two people come through it the same. I lost my husband seventeen years ago, and since then five other close members of my family have also died. And so I have come to understand a little more clearly the meaning of grief and how little prepared most of us are to cope with it.

I was already a Christian before my husband's death and the family had close connections with our local parish church. Bereavement put our faith to many tests, but it survived them all. Our shared experience has drawn us all closer to each other, although we are all now separated, physically.

In this book, I have drawn heavily on personal experience of the problems and difficulties—as well as some of the unexpected compensations—of widowhood and bringing up a family single-handed.

THE FIRST FEW DAYS

When someone we love dies, particularly someone on whom we have depended, one of our strongest emotions is likely to be sheer panic. We feel helpless. We don't know what to do. Dimly, we are aware that 'arrangements' will have to be made but we don't know what they are or how to go about them.

The first step is to call the doctor. If you are Roman Catholic you will want to call your priest at the same time you call your doctor. You might also want to call your pastor immediately if you are Protestant and have close personal ties with your pastor. After the doctor has confirmed the death, you will want to call the undertaker of your choosing. If you do not know an undertaker, ask your clergyman or a friend to recommend one.

THE DEATH

First of all, it is necessary to have the death certificate. This will be issued by the doctor or the undertaker. The amount of information needed for this form and the details of filing the death with the county and state health departments varies from state to state. Your undertaker will take care of this for you or advise you how to go about it.

Your undertaker is also accustomed to filling out the forms that release government benefits to which you are entitled.

ANNOUNCING THE DEATH

The undertaker will arrange for any announcements to be inserted in newspapers and, if necessary, help you with the wording of these. Because newspapers view death announcements as a form of advertisement (they give people date and time of visiting hours and funerals), they must be paid for. This service, if you desire it, will be included in the undertaker's bill to you. Some newspapers distinguish between death notices and obituaries, considering the second to be a news item.

Bereaved children will almost certainly want to know, when they are older, what friends, colleagues and relatives wrote about their dead parent, while people outside the family usually welcome this opportunity to express their sympathy and sense of loss.

In some areas of the country the undertaker, as a rule, prints memorial cards which you will want to send to friends and family.

THE FUNERAL

The first step is to get in touch with an undertaker. He will want to know whether or not you want visiting hours. Closed or open casket? (A closed casket and a not-long-delayed burial may save you the expense of embalming.) Burial or cremation? Funeral or memorial service at the funeral home or at a church? Do you already own a cemetery plot? Will you want him to hire cars for the funeral? He will ask you about pall bearers, ask you about clothes for the deceased, and so forth. This isn't a situation where you need to worry that you might forget something.

Papers needed to collect benefits

- Birth certificates of surviving spouse and minor children
- Marriage certificate—if spouse and minor children still live
- A certified copy of the death certificate for each benefit claimed
- Veteran's discharge papers
- Most recent federal income tax return or W-2 for Social Security record
- Paid invoice or receipt for funeral home expenses

Death benefits

- Social Security pays a small lump-sum death benefit to a qualified surviving spouse or the person responsible for paying funeral costs. The deceased must have worked under the Social Security system for ten years or for one and one half out of the three years prior to death
- Social Security pays qualifying dependents and survivors monthly benefits
- Honorable veterans are entitled to a small lump-sum death benefit, a grave headstone, and casket flag. Qualified veterans, some spouses and dependents, may be entitled to free burial in a national cemetery
- Workmen's Compensation Insurance pays benefits in some cases of on-the-job deaths
- Employer's benefits—vacation time
- Life and casualty insurance
- Credit unions, labor unions, fraternal organizations may have death benefits
- Civilian government workers who die may leave some survivor's benefits

The funeral director's reputation has been built on his concern with details and his ability to make things run smoothly.

● burial
gravestone is a permanent
  memorial
symbolizes being laid to rest
follows biblical tradition

but
burial is very costly
grave needs tending

● cremation
much cheaper than burial
symbolizes purifying release
ecologically sound—saves land for
  the living
no grave to look after

but
some dislike the idea of being
  burned
historically has pagan associations
often no visible memorial

COSTS

Funeral costs vary greatly, according to how simple or elaborate the funeral. As disrespectful as it may seem, ask the undertaker specific questions about costs and services. Ask for an itemized list of what he will charge and for what service, then decide whether or not you want each of the items and go over the list with him, subtracting any that don't suit your wishes. For instance, if embalming and viewing is not really important to you, ask for the difference in the costs between open casket and closed casket and then make your decision. The selection of a casket makes a big difference in a final invoice. Ask to see the whole range of caskets and liners. If you see cremation as an alternative, ask questions about it. The average cost of an American funeral/burial exceeds $2,500, whereas cremation costs rarely exceed $500.

THE FUNERAL SERVICE

A generation ago, most funerals took place in a church, but now most Protestant funerals take place in the funeral home. The actual form of the service will depend on your denomination or the denomination of the pastor who performs the ceremony. If you have no pastor, the funeral director will engage one for you. You may prefer to have a memorial service at which the body is not present.

Roman Catholic funerals are held in churches. There the family of the deceased and the coffin process in right before the service is to start and the family follows the coffin out of the church at the close of the funeral mass.

MUSIC

Some funerals include music. Often, a hymn which was a favorite of the dead person is sung, but, if you are not sure which to choose, the clergy will usually be able to suggest one or two. Funeral hymns need not always be slow and sad—the Christian hope is that there is new life after death and this positive approach can be reflected in brighter hymns than are often considered suitable for this occasion.

If the funeral is in a funeral home and you do not want any congregational singing or soloist, all the music played (before the funeral) may well be taped. An organist is sometimes provided if you desire special music, although many funeral homes do not have organs.

A short address may be given during the service recalling the life of the dead person, but many clergy prefer to use the prayers to thank God for his/her character and example, to commit him/her to God's love and to ask for comfort and peace for those who mourn.

DISPOSAL OF THE BODY

If the funeral service is to be followed by burial, the mourners will be taken to the burial ground for the final, very short, committal ceremony at the grave. From there, they will return to the house or else go their way, according to the arrangements they have made.

Most graves, these days, are marked by a simple headstone which can be erected any time after two months or so, once the ground has settled. More elaborate memorials will have to wait for nine to twelve months.

If the death takes place in the middle of winter and the ground is frozen, the burial is often held in the spring. Family members may then attend and take part in a committal ceremony, or they may choose to leave the disposition in the hands of the funeral director. State laws vary as to the allowable disposition of ashes after the ceremony.

SIGNIFICANCE OF THE FUNERAL

Every bereaved person dreads this ordeal, but, whatever form this final ceremony takes, from a psychological point of view it is most important. Even quite young children should be included in this public act of mourning.

The funeral helps to impress the fact that death *has* taken place and the need to come to terms with what has happened. Much comfort is drawn from the gathering together of family, friends and neighbors. It brings home the reality of the situation when the mind is still numb enough to be protected from all the implications. The funeral marks the end of a brief period where all seems unreal, and is an essential part of mourning.

COPING WITH GRIEF

An understanding doctor will, if asked, give you something to help you through the day but it is unwise to expect any drug to be anything more than a temporary solution. After the death of her husband, a widow in public life was quoted as saying, 'Widows should be allowed to experience the grief of losing their husbands and widowers their wives without being treated with sleeping-pills and tranquillizers.' She felt sure that it is better for anyone who mourns to get grief out of the system while everyone around is being kind and helpful.

I myself feel it is better to live through a time of misery and sadness with a relatively clear head and as much dignity as one can muster, trying to realize that some aspects of life *are* tragic and have to be accepted. Most people would recover their balance and composure more quickly if doctors and well-meaning relatives would allow them to be thoroughly miserable for a time. This is the normal and healing reaction to sorrow and loss.

However upsetting it may be to other people to see the distress of mourners at a funeral, they should try to see also that grief and tears are natural and be glad that nature is taking a hand in the healing process.

Many people find a cup of tea particularly comforting. The body loses moisture through crying, so it is good to drink more than usual. Don't be afraid to take an aspirin if you get a headache from the tension—they won't cause any dependence. The more you take care of your physical needs, the fewer problems you will have.

THE WILL

As soon as possible after the death, those appointed to be responsible for the distribution of the dead person's belongings, known in legal language as the executors, should get together. They should arrange to see a lawyer and ask him to obtain probate. This is the legal name for transferring all the dead person's property to them, so that they can then distribute it on the dead person's behalf. This process is known as 'proving a will' and should not take more than a few weeks, depending on how complicated or how simple the will is, and on how fast the lawyer works.

THE LAWYER
The choice of a lawyer is up to the executors, and they should ask him for a rough estimate of his fees before engaging him to

do the job. If the executors are not satisfied with the amount, they are quite at liberty to shop around.

Lawyers are there to help you, and will answer any queries you may have in terms which you will understand. They will tell you that no part of the dead person's estate (everything that he/she owned) can be distributed until the will has been validated. They will explain what this means and how if affects you.

NO WILL

They will also help you if you find that the person has, as far as you can see, died without making a will. This is termed 'intestacy'. In this situation the relatives should gather together all the information they can about what the person owned, his estate, and take all the documents they can find to the lawyer. There are certain rules laid down by law to cover intestacy, and usually the husband or wife will inherit the estate.

OTHER CASES

Sometimes the dead person will have made his will without the help of a lawyer. In this case, the executors, if there are any, should take the will to a lawyer as soon as possible after the death, so that he can try to obtain probate. There are many legal pitfalls which someone making his own will may have fallen into, so it is always advisable to go to a lawer when you want to make a will (see section headed 'Preparing for bereavement').

If you (or any close relative of the dead person) feel that you have been treated unfairly in the will, you should write to the lawyer and tell him as soon as possible. You may find that you can appeal to the court for the will to be changed in your favor.

HOW LONG?

So long as there are not too many complications, an estate can usually be wound up within six months of the death. When a business is involved it may take longer. The cost varies considerably, and will, or course, depend on how long it takes the lawyer to sort it all out. His fee will usually come out of the estate.

BELONGINGS

One of the most difficult tasks to tackle after a death is the disposal of the dead person's clothes and effects. It is best done as soon as possible. If you can't face it alone, ask a member of the family or a close friend to help you with it. The longer you put it off, the more you will dread it and it will be at the back of your mind all the time.

At all costs, resist the temptation to 'make a shrine' of the room or chair or workbench. A century ago, it was a common custom to leave everything as it had been, to behave as though the dead person would be coming back and to try to maintain a relationship which no longer existed. Many lives have been cramped and stunted by this attitude to death. By all means keep and treasure some things which have special signficance and provide happy memories, but best give the rest away.

There will be some items which you may want certain people to have, such as a piece of jewelry or a fountain pen, which you know they will treasure too and keep as a memento. Of the remainder, clothing, books or furniture are always needed by various voluntary organizations who will usually arrange for them to be collected and who will, no doubt, give you a receipt for your contribution upon request.

UNDERSTANDING DEATH

WHAT IS DEATH?

Nothing perplexes people more than death. It seems a strange, unnatural disaster that makes us aware we have no power, in the end, to control our own lives. What does it mean? Why should it happen? How can we best face up to it?

THE BODY DIES

Looked at medically, there is nothing unnatural about death. Throughout life the parts of the body continually repair themselves, but as we get older these repairs are not as successful as they used to be, and at last the vital organs break down. Similarly the body's repair systems may not be able to cope when it is harmed by disease or severe injury. The heart stops beating, breathing ceases and—the final, irreversible step—the brain no longer functions. Then life has departed and cannot be brought back.

MORE THAN A BODY

It is hard to believe that when the body dies the person no longer exists, though some think so. Despite the mystery of death, most people find it rings true that the human personality is more than just the body and that in some way we must pass through death.

There have been many different beliefs about what actually happens. Some have thought that man has an immortal soul which at death is freed from the hindrances of the body. Some believe that the dying person is taken into God and merged with the divine, losing his identity. Hinduism and other Eastern faiths teach reincarnation—that after death people are reborn as another baby or an animal, and so on over and over again.

A WHOLE PERSON

Christians believe that we are more than just bodies. But we are not immortal spirits living in our bodies like snails in their shells, so that at death we can discard the useless body with relief. We are whole people, a unity of body and spirit. My body is me, not a shell; my personality is expressed through my body.

BIBLICAL STATEMENTS ABOUT DEATH

● If our hope in Christ is good for this life only and no more, then we deserve more pity than anyone else in all the world. But the truth is that Christ has been raised from death, as the guarantee that those who sleep in death will also be raised.

● Our brothers, we want you to know the truth about those who have died, so that you will not be sad, as are those who have no hope. We believe that Jesus died and rose again, and so we believe that God will take back with Jesus those who have died believing in him.

● Jesus said to Martha, 'I am the resurrection and the life. Whoever believes in me will live, even though he dies; and whoever lives and believes in me will never die.'

SEPARATION

So there *is* something unnatural about death. It separates the personality from the body, which were meant to be closely joined. And, as the bereaved know only too well, death separates you from those you love. The anguish and horror of death show that it is an enemy of mankind.

The Bible makes sense of all this by explaining that death is the result of mankind's disobeying God and ignoring him. It is the final stage in a separation even worse than the others—the separation of each of us from God. That is a kind of 'death' even while we're alive.

NEW LIFE IN JESUS

So Christians look at death realistically and don't try to say it doesn't matter. They recognize how dreadful it is. They realize we also have a source of hope—Jesus Christ, who was executed on a cross but who was raised back to life by God. Everyone who trusts in him can have the assurance that after death he will be with Jesus.

Because Jesus died for us, we need no longer be separated from God. And when he rose again from death it was to a new life in which we too can share. Because that new life is imperishable, death is now a gateway to an even closer friendship with God. It is a deep comfort to those left behind to know that death can't separate them for ever from those who have died, because in Christ they will be reunited.

THE RESURRECTION OF THE BODY

The Christian idea of heaven is not a place where immortal souls float around! Although death does separate the personality from the body for a time, in Jesus they will be joined again. After all, Jesus himself was raised from death physically, with a real body, not as a ghost. Christians believe that when this world's time is up, the bodies of all who have died will be raised. We shall be judged by God as whole people, and believers will have an unimaginably full life with God for ever.

NO LONGER UNBEARABLE

And so death loses its terror for those who believe the Christian good news. It is still solemn, and undeniably sad, but our hope makes it bearable. This isn't wishful thinking, either, for it is based on God's strength and love which he had demonstrated by raising Jesus.

REALIZATION

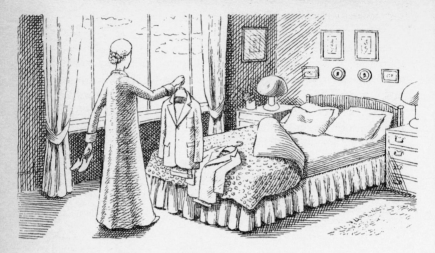

DEATH OF A PARENT

When a parent dies, we nearly always experience feelings of guilt and remorse. We reproach ourselves for not appreciating them more when they were alive, for not visiting them more often, for not doing more to help them. We remember our unkindness or impatience.

If Grandma or Grandpa had grown difficult with age and were living with us in a small house, we may remember the times we half-wished they'd die or that someone else would look after them. Now that this wish has been granted, we may torment ourselves with regret. We wish we could call them back and say, 'I didn't mean it'.

Many sons, going back to the room or house where a parent had passed the final years of life, realize with shame what a difference another coat of paint would have made and how little time it would have taken to do.

IN PROPORTION
It is important to realize that such regrets are natural and that the dead parent may well have felt impatience, annoyance and

exasperation with us. Family life includes conflict as well as love. We have to accept remorse as part of our mourning, not glossing over past attitudes but giving them greater significance than they deserve.

There will have been faults on both sides, and in earlier days, under less trying circumstances, no doubt both people would have flared up, calmed down and even had a good laugh over the very things which just now strike us as unforgivable. Such emotions will, of course, go all the deeper and be more tormenting in the rare cases where the dead person has committed suicide.

GOD'S FORGIVENESS

The Christian response to distressing memories of things done and left undone is to offer up our conflicting emotions to God, our heavenly Father. He knows our temperaments and family characteristics and what the pressures were. We can thank him for our parents and all they did for us; we can remember the good times and ask forgiveness for the bad, reminding ourselves that the love which enables us to make allowances for our own children is a reflection of *his* love which understands and forgives us.

While people are still alive, there is always time to put things right, but death is final and robs us of that opportunity. But if, when they are no longer with us, we now think only with love towards the person we have neglected or misunderstood, and if we can learn from our experience to do everything we can for those who are still with us, then gradually these feelings of guilt will lessen and we shall be comforted.

HELPING OTHERS

Many old people today live alone and far away from their families. Many of them would enjoy better health and spirits if they could be included in the activities of another family near at hand. Helping others is a sure way of helping ourselves, and many people whose own parents have died find satisfaction in befriending a lonely grandparent or a single parent and involving them in their normal family life.

DEATH OF A CHILD

This is one of the most bitter forms of bereavement. It seems all wrong, unnatural and, for the child, completely undeserved. A real part of ourselves has been torn from us.

REAL LOVE

Much similar guilt and remorse will be felt, but again we need to remind ourselves that impatience, cross words, misunderstandings are all part of family life. Children know when genuine love exists. They soon recognize that it is love which prompts what may seem to them harsh or unjust behavior on the part of parents.

Children see things in black and white and do not hold grudges. They thrive better on clashes where love is, than on indifference or total freedom to do as they like without love. One little girl arrived at school, sobbing bitterly. When the teacher asked her what was wrong, she said, 'Mummy doesn't love me—she never says, "Mind the road!"'

A VALUABLE LIFE

Although Christian parents will be as shattered by their child's death as anyone else, it is, I think, a little easier to accept because a belief in a future life gives a proportion and perspective to this one. We are all locked up in our ideas of time, but for God time is unimportant. This means that a short and, to our minds, tragically incomplete life is just as valid and valuable to him as one of seventy or eighty years.

The Ultimate Loss: Coping with the Death of a Child by Joan Bordow (Beaufort Books, 9 East 40th St, New York, NY 10016) is well worth its $12.95 price. From personal experience the author shows how to walk through grief to character growth and spiritual awakening. Also includes addresses of support groups.

Renowned psychiatrist Elisabeth Kübler-Ross's book *On Children and Death* (Macmillan, New York NY) is most likely in your local library.

ON LOAN

We all want what is best for those we love, but what we think is best for them may not always be in their long-term interest. If we believe that children are on loan from God, it becomes easier to understand that he loves them far more than we ever could, and will never let them slip from him. As events sometimes turn out, it may even become possible to be thankful that they were not called upon to face some disease or disaster which may have demanded more from them than they would have been able to give.

There is no glib or easy answer to the 'Why?' of the death of a child. Our reassurance must lie in the conviction that Jesus, who said 'Let the children come to me', will hold them in life and death and keep them safe.

SAFE FOR EVER

Only God is perfect, so it isn't a surprise to realize that even children are spoiled by the wrongness of the world. They are weak, like everyone else, and as they grow older and more able to form their own opinions, they too have to establish their own values. The most important of these is to learn where God comes into our lives, and to love him. If we do love him, then to be with him, safe for ever, is the best thing we could ever wish for ourselves or our children. This is what Christians know as heaven.

In the baptism or dedication of our children we take on the responsibility of making decisions on their behalf. We promise to bring the children up in the Christian way.

However, God is more concerned about our inward relationship with him than for the outward ceremony. We can be assured that all children are especially dear to God, who is Love.

BROTHERS AND SISTERS

If there are other children in the family, the parents must look beyond their own grief. Brothers and sisters will need comfort, strength, patience and more love than ever. They must not be excluded from the emotions which will hit them just as hard, though in different ways. It is important that the neighborhood, shocked by bereavement, does not add to their burden by conveying a sense of isolation. This can lead to an unconscious shunning of the bereaved family, people feeling that they will want to be left alone, and so the children will feel more bewildered or shut out than ever. They must always be allowed to grieve with their parents within the security of the family circle.

THE STILL-BORN CHILD

Many people think that a still-birth or the death of a baby a few days old does not cause the same grief as the loss of an older child. But the wounds are just as deep and painful. The bereaved mother should not be put in a ward with women nursing their live children but taken home as soon as medically possible to be comforted by relatives or friends and any other children she may have.

GRIEF AND FEARS

Many mothers of still-born children say that they have never 'got over' this experience. Times come when they relive the disappointment and wonder what the child would now be like had he or she lived.

The father usually has to go back to work after a few days, leaving the mother at home, still weak and emotional. This is when support from neighbors and friends is most necessary. Usually, the mother's most pressing need will be to talk about what has happened. She may need to voice fears about her next baby being still-born; to express her feelings of guilt; that the doctors had let her down; even that, without a child to nurse, her health may suffer. The greatest help will be to lend a sympathetic but practical ear.

What about the father of a still-born child? His grief will be just as great and his frustrations perhaps greater. He has a knife-twisting duty of registering the death at the same time as the birth, and having to make arrangements which will spare the mother, such as putting away the baby clothes and the cradle.

FUNERAL

After any bereavement, the funeral is very important, even in the case of a very young child. Simply to take away the baby hinders rather than helps the parents to adjust to its death. Some parents are not even told what has happened to their baby. This can prolong their agony. Such insensitivity does unfortunately happen in some hospitals. The parents need to mourn their loss openly at a funeral ceremony. They need to grieve, letting the tears which heal bitterness flow while strength returns.

MISCARRIAGE OR ABORTION

When a baby is growing inside the womb, the hormones, which are the body's chemical messengers, are telling the mother's body how to prepare for the birth. When this process is interrupted by the loss of the baby, the body is confused and takes a while to settle down.

During this time, you may well feel emotional and depressed. You may feel cheated out of having a baby and wonder why yours was lost. There is usually a very good reason for the body rejecting a baby before birth—often the baby is abnormal and might have grown up handicapped.

If you have chosen to have an abortion, you may have the added burden of feeling responsible for the death. This may be offset by the relief of not having an unwanted or a handicapped child, but at such a time feelings are inevitably mixed.

When you have lost a child in this way you may find yourself worrying about its spiritual future. One couple I know asked their minister to read the funeral service to them after a miscarriage and found this a great comfort.

DEATH OF HUSBAND OR WIFE

Every married couple has to face the fact that sooner or later one of them will die. It is estimated that one woman in five will be a widow before she is 60. For most people, these facts are too disturbing, and so, when the inevitable happens, the shock is all the greater.

Whether or not you take the Christian view of marriage, it is a fact that husband and wife become bound to each other in far more subtle ways than being mere parties to a contract. When your husband or wife dies, life loses its center so that you feel disorientated, off-balance, wounded.

In his widely-read book, *A Grief Observed*, C. S. Lewis wrote, 'No one ever told me that grief felt so like fear.' What will happen? we ask ourselves. What shall we do? Who will care? And, unlike the death of a parent or a child, this is one experience we have to face alone. Only those who have been through the same experience can be expected to understand.

For this reason, another widow or widower is probably the best person to turn to for help.

Suddenly you are back where you started—a single person but older than the last time round. Your marriage contract is ended; you must start a new life. The pangs of birth into this life will be there, but they will not last for ever, though at the time it may seem so.

Do not be afraid to ask another man or woman to teach you how to undertake the things your partner did in the marriage. If your husband always filled in your tax return there is sure to be a man you know who would be pleased to help you; or in the case of a widower, a woman who will be happy to show you how to mend a torn shirt.

NO EASY WAY

Never think you are alone in feeling as you do or that 'it's different for some'. It is certainly no easier for the Christian. In some ways, bereavement is harder, because Christians often feel that they should be able to overcome these emotions. They then worry because they feel they are not coping as well as they should. But one aspect *is* different for the Christian—belief in a future life and in the never-ending love of God makes it easier for the Christian to 'let go' of the one they loved.

This 'letting go' is all-important. Without it, we shall never fully recover our serenity and will be left with a sense of deep hopelessness. Making a shrine of the dead person's room, visits made too often to the grave, shutting out other people and other interests from our lives—all such refusals to 'let go' stunt our growth and would certainly not be what our partner would want for us. If it is true that the scars of bereavement never entirely disappear, it is just as true that if we do not let our dead go, the wounds will not heal.

EFFECTIVE FAITH

In the early days, following my husband's death, I dreaded the nights. I found then, as in other crises since, that I couldn't pray. Instead, familiar words from the Bible kept running through my mind—'I will never leave you; I will never abandon you'; 'in quietness and in trust shall be your strength'.

I was so thankful, then, to have had a Christian upbringing

—it seems to me that there can be no such thing as 'instant faith'; it has to be built up over the years slowly, until it imperceptibly becomes part of us. I've found that when life suddenly calls for the exercise of great faith, it's usually at a time when coherent thought—even prayer—is impossible. All I could ask was, 'Please don't let me be bitter.'

The question we have to put to ourselves is not the all-too-frequent 'Why should this happen to me?' but 'This happens to other people—why shouldn't it happen to me?' Death is universal; it comes to all and should never be thought of as a punishment from God.

God does not exempt us from death by changing the natural laws which he himself has made. When he became man as Jesus Christ, even he willingly accepted death for us, in order to destroy the power of death. The Christian promise is that as death could not hold him, so it does not have the final word over us or those we love.

WHEN A FRIEND DIES

It is often assumed that the 'worst' form of bereavement is the death of a husband or wife, but every bereavement is shattering in its own way.

The death of a friend brings a different but equally piercing sense of loss, especially in the case of two people who may have shared their lives since student days or who may have lived together loyally all their adult lives. The effects of the broken relationship will in many ways be the same as for a widow or widower, and made even more poignant because there will usually be no children to help, and because others may think one's grief out of place.

We tend to underestimate a person's grief for a dead friend. Even when close friends have been physically separated for many years, there is grief for the loss of early shared experiences and all the close ties which still bind them together uniquely.

COPING WITH GRIEF

It is perfectly normal for a bereaved person to be sad, withdrawn and tearful. It does not mean that he or she is depressive or neurotic. Normal, human experiences are not merely medical problems to be cured with pills, though these may help. Grief is like an illness, though, and can be disabling. Sometimes it produces physical symptoms of its own, and it doesn't help to ignore it. No matter how 'sensible' we imagine ourselves to be, our emotional behavior after the loss of someone close to us seems puzzling and frightening. It is possible to remain dry-eyed and apparently unmoved at the funeral and yet be undone by very little things.

THE PATTERN

After the first, numbing shock there comes a period of pining followed by mixed feelings of depression and apathy alternating with bursts of intense activity and, often, anger and despair.

HOW LONG?

Many mourners have cried, 'How long will it last?' It is
impossible to generalize. Within reason, any length of time is
'normal'. Such a fundamental adjustment has to be a gradual
process. A rough estimate would be a year or two, while we
learn to accept what has happened and to adapt to the
situation. After, say, two years, a drawn-out, disabling grief
suggests that medical help should be sought. Such a problem is
familiar to a doctor and he will be able to help you over the
depressive stage of your bereavement.

TIMETABLE OF GRIEF (the stages and their order vary, and may
overlap)

1 Shock	Muscular weakness, emptiness and inner tension
2 Numbness	Everything seems unreal and remote
3 Struggle between fantasy and reality	You find reality difficult to accept and may act partly as though it had not happened
4 Feelings of guilt, panic or frenzy	You may want to withdraw from the outside world and even your family
5 Depression	To be expected
6 Release	Shedding of tears or release of a flood of grief
7 Painful memories	You find yourself able to face memories and accept them
8 Acceptance	Your new life begins and plans for the future form. Practical and emotional problems become easier to deal with

---

WHAT ABOUT THE CHILDREN?

If your children are in need of more support than you can give
them at the moment, perhaps a relative, neighbor, or your
regular babysitter will help you out. Since they are already
uneasy about the loss of a loved one, it's best not to send them
out of town, where they will conjure up new fears of
abandonment.

It is better to be occupied than to sit about and worry. It will help the children if they are allowed to give a hand with any job they can do. To do things together gives everyone a sense of purpose and security. In all times of grief, habit can be a comfort—to go on doing the daily chores, peeling the potatoes, going to work, and the like.

UNDERSTANDING YOURSELF

No one who has not experienced bereavement can fully understand its conflicting emotions. It is like a second adolescence, with all the adolescent's swings of mood. You are over-sensitive to casual remarks; you dread waking up in the morning, especially at weekends when you imagine everyone else is having a good time. Everything becomes out of proportion: nothing seems as important as your own grief.

Most people discover that their restlessness comes from the instinct to look for the dead person; the hope that he or she hasn't really gone. One woman found herself needlessly rearranging a cupboard and turning out drawers before she recognized her deep need to 'find' her dead husband. Some try to 'bring back' the loved one by way of fantasies or speaking aloud to them as though they were in the room. Some experience vivid dreams; many of these recall happy events in the past but most have an underlying uneasiness.

VIVID MEMORIES

Equally common is the sharply-defined recollection of the events which led up to the death and the ability of the bereaved to recount every detail of the previous hours and days. It is as though time stood still just as a single moment is captured in a photograph.

You remember that it was the day the milkman was late or the day you missed the bus to work. One man, months later, was able to recite word for word a letter he had just read when the news of his wife's death was brought to him. Bereaved people will hang on to such details as a means of making their dead seem closer and still with them in the world.

FINDING YOUR WAY

We react differently according to our temperament, our upbringing, the people we are with and other less obvious causes. Some long to talk to anyone who will listen; others shut themselves away and talk within themselves; others will write it all down in the form of a diary or a letter to the one who has died.

There is no 'right' way of grieving—everyone has to work a way through by whatever method brings most relief and comfort. Although we can derive much help and insight from other people's experiences, in the end we all have to fight our own way through the jungle, making use of every bit of encouragement we can find.

WHAT TO EXPECT

The trouble is—we don't know what to expect! Death has probably never before come so close. It is a new experience and we don't know how to deal with it. A book like this can help by trying to explain what is happening and describing the emotions which are tearing you apart. Whatever your emotions may be, never be afraid of your own reactions to grief. Accept them, understand them, and you will be half-way to using them positively.

NUMBNESS
Remind yourself that you are in a state of emotional shock. Be thankful for the numbness which carries you through the first days or weeks, even though you know that feeling is bound to return—like the pain in frost-bitten fingers when they begin to thaw.

If possible, use this short break, when often the mind works clearly and competently on a practical level, to cope with the immediate problems, and thus prevent yourself losing confidence in your ability to manage on your own. But you should try not to make any far-reaching decisions until later: in your present state of mind your judgment will not be reliable.

THE SECOND STAGE
This is when many irrational fears and emotions come to the surface. These are entirely natural. People often feel physically ill, fear they are going mad or think they are about to have a

nervous breakdown. As they struggle to control the conflict inside them, all sorts of dreadful possibilities run through their minds. None of these imaginary disasters is likely to happen.

One of the greatest fears a young parent may have is that he or she will also die and leave the children orphaned. Dying of a 'broken heart' is not entirely unknown but it is extremely unlikely.

PHYSICAL SYMPTOMS

Sometimes, physical symptoms will attack the bereaved; these normally fade within a week or so without producing the real illness from which the dead person had suffered.

The day after my husband's funeral, I went to my doctor because one side of my face was swollen and inflamed and I was sure that I had 'caught' the same disease. The doctor assured me that I was perfectly healthy and that my face would soon return to normal. It did.

A young husband whose wife had died in pregnancy suffered for several days what could only be described as labor pains.

Many women who have lost a husband as a result of heart disease imagine that they are about to go the same way, not realizing that quickened heart-beats or palpitations are often the response to fear and anxiety.

The only thing which saves us from hypochondria is a sense of humor. Try to see the funny side of your reactions. I have thanked God for the laughter of family and friends.

Every bereaved person will experience some of the following physical and emotional symptoms:

insomnia	lack of concentration	fear of illness
trembling	itching skin	fear of breakdown
coldness	blurred vision	headaches
indigestion	difficulty in swallowing	dizziness
constipation	nervousness	diarrhoea
coughs and colds	depression	irritability
lapses of memory	panic	lack of interest
fatigue	anxiety	fullness in the throat
loss of appetite	sweating	

ANGER

One emotion which upsets and shocks many people is a feeling of extreme anger. Anger frequently goes with fear; an animal may be docile until something frightens it, when it will turn and attack.

For the bereaved person, the world has suddenly become a very frightening place, and one reaction is to fight back. Most people blame themselves in some measure for the death of someone near to them, and because this is too painful to bear they tend to take it out on someone else.

A widow will find many scapegoats on which to unload her anger at what life has thrown at her. One woman marched into her husband's office and accused his colleagues of not pulling their weight and leaving him to shoulder all the responsibility. Another blamed her doctor for making what she considered was a wrong diagnosis.

GRIEVANCE

There is often a deep sense of grievance. Life seems very unjust. Many blame God. 'How can he love us if he lets this happen?' they ask. 'What have we done to deserve this?' There is no need to feel guilty for voicing such thoughts. When doctors are the subject of wild accusations after bereavement, they do not let it affect their relationship with the patient. How much greater is God's understanding of our turmoil.

The greatest comfort we have is to know that we can take all our fears, resentment and anger to him, believing that such destructive emotions will dissolve in his love to be replaced by peace and hope. We don't become immune from tragedy if we believe in God, but we can be protected from bitterness and despair in our suffering by his strength and presence with us.

BITTERNESS

Bitterness is a destructive emotion which we must guard against. If we become bitter it will set up hostilities within the family on account of the cruel, unjust things we shall say. This is a time when we should be drawing strength from being united, but, sadly, it can also be a time when relationships are damaged beyond repair.

It should not be necessary to point out that a child must never be blamed for contributing to the death of a parent or a brother or sister. That would be too much for him to bear when he is already suffering under his own burden of grief.

For the same reason, it is thoughtless as well as stupid to vent one's anger on a close friend or relative. They, too, have been bereaved and will be feeling angry; if a situation develops beyond control, lasting divisions can result. Not only that—if we persist in unreasonable anger and reproaches, we drive other people away and find ourselves more bereft than ever.

● DESTRUCTIVE ATTITUDES	● CONSTRUCTIVE ATTITUDES
bitterness	accepting what has happened
despair	hopefulness
pride	faith in the future
shutting yourself away	making the most of what is left
self-pity	willingness to recover
looking for someone to blame	being thankful for the past
becoming a martyr	accepting help and friendship
cursing God	committing everything to God

HALLUCINATION

Another disconcerting effect of bereavement is a form of hallucination in which we 'see' the dead person. This can be so vivid that we find ourselves reaching out to touch him or her. This, too, is normal and becomes less frequent.

But it can be an agonizing disappointment to walk along a street, sure that the person in front is your dead relative. It may be just a way of walking, but the jolt is enough to pierce the heart and bring back all the pain. Even after so long, it still happens to me and I can only turn to Jesus, who knows what sadness and grief are like.

LETTING THEM GO

Letting go of our dead is the most difficult and yet the most important part of grief and mourning. Gradually we have to cut those ties which hold us back from making a new life for ourselves and the family. Memories must remain and be a source of comfort and thankfulness, but if we refuse to accept the fact of death we shall become stunted, unable to grow— surely this would not be what those who loved us would want to happen.

ASSOCIATIONS

Mercifully, the true realization of what we have lost comes only slowly, but each day will bring its reminders of the past. This pervading sadness was summed up by one widow who said, 'I keep thinking I must tell Jim about that when he gets home— and then I remember that I shan't be able to tell him anything ever again.'

Different associations bring pain to different people. A widower never set foot in his local pub after his wife died because they had always had their Saturday lunch there when she was alive. Another man wrote to his pastor and told him he intended joining another church because he felt he would always 'see' his wife in the pew they had always occupied, and he felt he must begin a new church life in a different building.

Although I can hardly believe now that it took so long, my diary tells me that it was four years before I could listen to a record or go to a concert. I do remember, though, that the tears which accompanied the music when I did feel able to hear it again were peaceful rather than painful, and I knew that another stage of my own mourning had passed.

If you have lived with someone for a long time, it makes it all the more difficult to take decisions and make changes you know your partner would probably have disapproved of or disliked. There was a man I used to visit; his wife had recently died and his sons wanted him to have a television set. 'No,' he said, 'Emmy didn't approve of television.' Nothing would move him. Unfortunately, Emmy hadn't been too keen on the radio, either, so his evenings must have been long and lonely.

However, in the end he was persuaded to have a set, though obviously feeling very guilty about it.

ACCEPTANCE

To accept what has happened demands two things—time and the willingness to recover. You have to learn how much you can take at a time. There is nothing so tiring as strong emotion and the bereaved person is often very tired indeed. You must learn how much you can bear of the company of certain people, well-meaning though they may be. Do not push yourself. Above all, never feel inadequate or defeated when you have to give in for a while.

Some days you feel more able to do things than others, so it is only sensible to press ahead then and not to attempt too much on the bad days. This gradual adjustment to life will enable you to regain your balance and perspective. The numb period at the beginning of mourning gives the needed breathing-space to come to terms with changed circumstances. Realization dawns slowly, different aspects become more clear, the future begins to shape itself. Look at each new problem squarely and deal with it only when it happens—not before.

Within the family, all the members can help each other. How about giving an award to the one who can make the others laugh, however shakily!

ANXIETY

It is quite natural for you to feel that you cannot cope, and that the problems and worries of everyday life are threatening to overwhelm you. Try to live one day at a time, and not to look too far into the future.

The Bible has some sound advice for dealing with anxiety:

● 'So do not worry about tomorrow; it will have enough worries of its own. There is no need to add to the troubles each day brings.' The Gospel of Matthew

● 'Don't worry about anything, but in all your prayers ask God for what you need, always asking him with a thankful heart. And God's peace, which is far beyond human understanding, will keep your hearts and minds safe in union with Christ Jesus.' Paul's letter to the Philippians

IS THERE ANYBODY THERE?

It is easy to understand why the savage separation which death brings makes some people turn to spiritualism in an effort to make contact with the ones they have lost. Every bereaved person longs to speak to them just once more and to know if they are 'all right'.

But, to my mind, this reveals a selfish element in our love. Instead of letting them go, we are trying to bind them to an earthly existence when they have been set free to continue their journey in a new place and time-scale. Instead of allowing them to go forward, we are trying to hold them back. Is it really love or is it self-concern on our part? Are we putting our sorrow before their new opportunities?

For a Christian, this attempt to keep them here on earth, where we know what is going on, shows a lack of trust in a loving God. He is Father of us all and loves us all equally, so we can safely commit our dead into his safe keeping, remembering that he has also promised strength and guidance for those left behind. We need fear neither for them nor for ourselves.

This sounds all very fine in theory but is no defense against the pangs of mourning we all suffer . . . but, we are not alone —God bears our cross with us. As we pass through this painful experience with him for company, we discover on the other side that the end of the way is joy. And joy is stronger than suffering because beyond the cross is the resurrection.

The book *Mourning Song* by Joyce Landorf (Fleming Revell, Old Tappan, NJ) may be of great help to any mourner.

DO YOU WANT TO RECOVER?

When we lose someone we have loved deeply and relied on, life loses most of its purpose. All our emotional energies are directed towards grieving for that person and our own loss. We are knocked sideways, unable to face the world. But sooner or later we have to make a fresh start. The longer the period of mourning has been, the more courage it will take to risk being hurt by life again.

Some people take refuge in 'I don't feel very well' or 'no one would want me!' Others, having become used to sympathy, forbearance and—dare I say it?—the limelight, find they do not want to rejoin the rat race.

TURNING POINTS

Another obstacle which some people find at the start of their new life is a sense of disloyalty to the dead person. They feel it is wrong when they occasionally experience a pang of joy. They feel ashamed when they find they have forgotten their grief when they are with friends.

But this is how it should be. He or she wasn't at the forefront of your mind every minute of every day when alive; neither should he be now. These times of forgetting, happiness even, are to be welcomed. They show that true healing is well under way.

One woman said she knew the worst was over when she was able to take the car to the mechanic without even thinking that this was a job her husband would have done.

Slowly, the piercing pain of grief will give place to the dull ache of mourning and then to lengthening periods of calm when memories bring more happiness than sorrow. You will know, then, that all is well.

TAKE STOCK

This is the time to take stock.

- consider new interests
- get in touch with old friends
- make plans—however restricted they may have to be
- don't make loneliness a way of life—that would be a poor tribute to the person you have lost

Take stock of yourself, as well. Respect your body and mind when they tell you you have overdone things. If you are tired, have a rest and clean the house later. If you are holding down a job and keeping the family together, don't be too proud to accept any offer of help during the week so that you will have more time to spend with the children at the weekend.

There will still come days when nothing seems worthwhile, or there's no one to do anything for, or you think 'Who cares, anyway?' It helped me to recall the medieval philosophy that the smallest thing done well—arranging a vase of flowers, carving a piece of wood, weeding a flower-bed— anything which adds to the goodness and beauty of the world satisfies the worker and gives glory to the Creator.

MOURNING

Grief is what we experience after bereavement: mourning is the way in which we express it. Mourning is of the utmost importance because it is the working out of grief. To bottle it up is a great mistake.

RITUALS AND CONVENTIONS

One hundred years ago the whole community would be affected by a death. Blinds were drawn in the house of the bereaved family and in the windows of houses along the route taken by the funeral procession. Black crêpe ribbons hung on the doors. When the hearse passed by, people stood still or raised their hats and lowered their eyes. Relatives dressed in black, used black-edged paper for their letters, wore veils in public, stayed indoors for a time and cancelled all social engagements for several months. Society recognized that mourners were people with a special role in the life of the community.

SECURITY

Much of this seems to us, now, an excessive and morbid attitude to death, but it had its advantages. The mourners, in particular, knew what was expected of them and it gave them security in a world which had tumbled about their ears. They knew the part they had to play and as the prescribed period of mourning slipped away, so, usually, did their own grief.

A definite pattern of mourning was comforting to conform to and in most cases it 'worked'. Gradual physical emergence into the world again coincided with gradual emotional emergence as well. The rites and customs had been observed; life could continue.

THE MODERN TABOO

Today, we are less willing to face the fact of death. True, certain rituals are observed, at least in the first few days. We write to the family concerned, send flowers, ask if we can do anything to help. Then we try to dismiss the whole subject from our minds—it strikes too near home and makes us fear for ourselves.

The modern attitude to grief makes it much more difficult to mourn adequately. We have been indoctrinated with the idea that to mourn for longer than a week or two shows a weakness of will, if not sheer self-indulgence. Because death is nowadays a forbidden subject, it is more difficult to impress on those who do not understand that, far from being morbid or thoughtless, mourning is a psychological necessity.

GOING TO THE FUNERAL

No one enjoys going to a funeral. It is distressing to see the grief of those who mourn, but the sympathy of neighbors and the respect for grief has tremendous value in supporting the bereaved within a comforting framework of convention.

The vast majority of mourners derive much consolation from the service itself. The words seem to stick in their minds and come back to them in the weeks that follow. A widower told the minister after his wife's funeral, 'It said all the things I couldn't say myself.' A widow explained how surprised she had been to see so many in church: 'I felt so proud of him . . . all those people . . . they must have thought the world of him.'

LOOSE ENDS

The funeral is the last service (in both senses) that we do for our dead, but I believe it is of even greater service to the living. It ties up the loose ends of the life which is over; it reassures us that we have done everything necessary on a practical plane. 'We gave him a good send-off, didn't we?' was how one widow put it. 'It tidies everything up,' said another, 'now I feel I can start again—a bit like Monday morning.'

SIGHING AND CRYING

There's nothing like a good cry. Sighing and crying are the most obvious and most understandable expressions of grief, and doctors agree that if we repress these two outlets, or are denied them by others, we are more likely to become disturbed later on. This is borne out by the case of a man who showed no outward sign of grief after his wife's death but some years later, after visiting her sick sister in the same hospital, suffered a nervous breakdown.

NATURAL SORROW

For a while, we have to let ourselves down lightly and not fight to keep up appearances or conform to attitudes demanded by modern society.

I remember at the time of the Six Days' War in Israel seeing newspaper photographs of Jewish and Arab women sobbing uncontrollably, their faces crumpled and twisted by the intensity of their grief. Many readers of that paper wrote to the editor complaining that it was wrong for outsiders to see such sorrow. I could understand that they felt the press coverage was an intrusion, but I thought, as I looked at those women, 'How right they are to give full expression to their feelings. This is the real work of mourning—they will come through.' And, supported by the sympathy and prayers of people thousands of miles away, I think they did.

BAD TASTE

But not everyone is able to let themselves go in this way. Older people, brought up in times when it was considered bad taste to show any strong emotion, will often hold themselves on a very tight rein.

I was recently at the funeral of an elderly man; his widow was quietly crying and her sister leaned across and said loudly, 'Stop it, Elizabeth, everyone's looking at you.' Later, that widow bitterly resented the fact that even more attention had been focused on her and had made it impossible for her to 'take the funeral in'.

> 'We don't really want grief, in its first agonies, to be prolonged: nobody could. But we want something else of which grief is a frequent symptom, and then we confuse the symptom with the thing itself. I wrote the other night that bereavement is not the truncation of married love but one of its regular phases—like the honeymoon. What we want is to live our marriage well and faithfully through that phase too. If it hurts (and it certainly will) we accept the pains as a necessary part of this phase. We don't want to escape them at the price of desertion or divorce . . . We will still be married, still in love. Therefore we shall still ache. But we are not at all—if we understand ourselves—seeking the aches for their own sake.'
>
> **A Grief Observed**, C. S. Lewis

BARRIERS

Mourners who suffer most are those who are surrounded by relatives or friends with whom they cannot be natural. Some parents find it impossible to talk about the death with their children; some feel, mistakenly, that the children must be shielded from grief. Some cannot turn to elderly parents for help because they don't want to upset them. Some have quarrelled with their parents or their in-laws and have no point of contact with them any more.

Many women, having fought long and hard to establish a reputation for self-sufficiency and competence in a man's world, dare not now 'let themselves down' as they call it or admit that they are not invincible or possessed of unassailable self-control.

MANLY GRIEF

Men can be particularly hard hit in bereavement because of the traditional 'stiff upper lip' attitude which most have been taught to assume. Few allow themselves to cry in public. Many feel they cannot do so even within the family and suffer accordingly. But boys, in particular, benefit from seeing their father's tears.

Imagine the conflict in a lad who imagines it is unmanly to cry and yet whose most urgent need is to release his desperation in this way. He may well be surprised, even shocked, to see his own father cry, but will also learn that there is nothing wrong in the natural expression of grief and that tears at such a time have dignity and worth. Father and son can then grieve together and comfort each other.

If you repress every emotion, you create a barrier around yourself which no one can penetrate. It shuts you in and keeps other people out. You condemn yourself to suffer alone—and that is loneliness indeed.

SOLIDARITY

The same expressions of grief which can drive people away from those who mourn can also be a means of drawing together those chiefly concerned. Children should be allowed to join in the tears of bereaved parents. In the early stages, tears come frequently and unexpectedly, but soon a pattern of recovery begins to form—the one who stops crying first comforts the others and you all continue with the task in hand.

WHAT WILL IT MEAN?

WHO AM I?

We all need someone to love who loves us, and when a close relationship is broken we feel painfully alone. A widow who lost her husband, her mother and her sister, all within a year, explained, 'I don't feel special any more. I miss being cherished.'

Many married people tend to think alike on most things, so when one of them dies, it is as though half the other dies with them, and therefore half the assurance, half the security.

LOSS OF YOUR ROLE

Provided the bereaved family is not suffering actual hardship, the afflictions are mainly psychological. One bewildered woman said, 'You feel as though you were in a train which has gone on and left you in a siding.'

Something we have to guard against is getting used to living on the edge of other people's lives, reading about and listening to what everyone else is doing but taking no steps to join in.

You have lost your role in life. After the death of a husband, most women find they are now the head of the family, and it stops them in their tracks. Instead of being a husband, a man is now a widower and, however young, somehow pathetic.

UNNERVING

Most marriages exist within a framework of sharing, more so now when wives and husbands are often both at work and arrange between them the jobs to be done. So it is quite unnerving when a widow has to tackle 'his' jobs for the first time.

Take the mail delivery—if the bills were previously dealt with by the husband. In the early days of my widowhood, I felt guilty about opening letters addressed to my husband and some days found myself putting them on one side 'for when he comes home'. Other days, I used to stare at the envelopes and think, 'Who is Mr V. B. Richardson? He doesn't exist.'

At parties, people often ask 'What does your husband do?' and when I say that he's dead they rarely ask 'What do you do?' How do they think widows live these days without doing something, I wonder! So a widow often asks herself 'Who am I?'

LIFE WITHOUT A PARTNER

On the domestic front, it is undoubtedly harder to be a widower than a widow. Elderly men cannot imagine the rest of their lives without the one with whom they had shared everything. And younger men often feel inadequate when faced with running a home and bringing up children.

However, a man does have his job, which helps him take his mind off things while he is at work. It is also much easier for a man to remarry, however many children he has.

WIDOWS

The problems facing widows are also highly alarming. Among them are bewilderment, fear of breakdown, of financial difficulties, and of being pushed into the background by people generally.

The modern family has become much more self-contained than the old extended family all living within easy reach. Husbands and wives have come to rely only on each other, and even when the wife has a job of her own, her husband's death will seriously cut back what she does.

It takes time to learn to speak in the singular instead of the plural. You still hear yourself saying, 'Borrow our car' or 'Come round to our house'. In the case of wives who have become almost dependent on 'what my husband says', fear may assume panic proportions. However, there are people to give advice and organizations that help.

SECOND ADOLESCENCE

It is surprising how like a teenager you feel as a result of bereavement. There are the same unpredictable moods, the same periods of lethargy followed by bouts of over-activity, the same enthusiasms which fizzle out, the same hopes drowned in the same despairs. Other bereaved people have told me that they felt humiliated by such juvenile emotions and fought them violently.

In the same way that an adolescent isn't always sure where he fits in, the bereaved person finds it difficult to decide into which age-group he or she falls. This is especially true of the middle-aged. You haven't the same footing as grandparents; yet you are out of touch with young parents. You have little in common with single people whose lifestyle has been quite different. In addition, a widow often feels that being 'just a housewife' is no longer satisfying.

SOME HELPFUL ORGANIZATIONS

● National Association for Widowed People PO Box 3564 Springfield, Ill. 62708
Toll free hotline: 1-800-423-1100
In Illinois: 1-800-648-1100
This membership association has local chapters which provide support, magazine, newsletters, group travel.

● American Association of Retired Persons—Widowed Persons Service
1909 K St NW
Washington, DC 20049

Their help and information pack is a life-saver for all widowed people, not just those who are retired.

● Theos Foundation
11609 Frankstown Road
Pittsburgh, Pa. 15235
This is a Christian ministry attempting to help the bereaved, especially widows of preretirement age. One hundred and fifty local chapters provide support. Literature and seminars available.

WHO DO THEY THINK I AM?

I once read an article by a young widow who said, 'Being reduced to single living again is a horrible state—other people look on you as an emotional cripple and a second-class person.'

HUMILIATIONS

When a woman loses her husband (and, to a lesser degree, when a man loses his wife) other people are as confused by her change of status as she is.

Western society inflicts many humiliations on single people. A widow is only half a pair—she makes an uneven number at a table; she tends to stick out like a sore thumb and, worse still, is a constant reminder that any of those with her may be in her position one day. Men are more fortunate, here, as there is a shortage of single men and a man can more easily find someone to accompany him.

It is essential to cultivate a sense of humor in order to survive the slights and thoughtless suggestions which will come your way. A friend told me, 'Acquaintances will cross the road rather than speak to you—it's as though they'd seen a Martian with antennae and green scales.'

Another widow described how she swung between laughter and tears when people met her in the street and asked 'Are you feeling better now?' as though she'd had a nasty attack of flu.

NEGLECTED OR SUSPECTED

Fears that you may be forgotten or written off are not without foundation. A widow tends to be asked round for a cup of tea rather than to supper.

You feel you are now deemed fit only for female company: there is a widespread suspicion that all widows are husband-hunting. The sudden loss of masculine company is a deprivation for widows of all ages.

At a time when nerve-endings are raw and exposed, it isn't easy to be brave and make yourself vulnerable to heartache. Like it or not, however, it is essential to fight your way back into your circle of friends. But we must make allowances for those who cannot possibly understand what bereavement means . . . yet. We must learn to laugh at the ridiculous side of many situations in which we find ourselves.

A NEW START

Any form of deep suffering makes or breaks us. The experience of millions who have been through it is that when we feel most broken, that is the point from which we can start again. Every bereaved person is diminished, but faith can build us up once more. A widow told me, 'I can only keep going by reminding myself that I still matter to God and that I'm still important to him.'

REGAINING STRENGTH

The chief emotion of anyone meeting a bereaved person for the first time is one of acute embarrassment. They don't want to upset you and they don't know what to say. Above all, they dread a public display of tears. In the past, many of us will have felt the same so we can understand their wariness.

MAKING THE FIRST MOVE

We learn that, hard though it is, it is up to us to make the first move. We have to be the ones to go up to an acquaintance in the supermarket and say hello. Once the ice has been broken, we no longer find ourselves playing hide and seek among the baked beans and we can talk more normally.

News will get round that you have neither been struck dumb nor made mentally deficient—two conditions often absurdly associated with bereavement! Some people will be over-bracing and treat you as they would a child recovering from mumps. Some will speak in hushed voices and urge you to rest. But everyone means well and is doing their best—our part is to be grateful and to help them out.

Starting again is an exhausting business. Now, it's you who have to make all the running to keep in touch with people. In a world geared to couples, it becomes a battle to see yourself as a person in your own right, and to persuade others to do so.

JOIN IN

Gradually, you will receive invitations again. However little you feel like accepting them, make the effort because, otherwise, people's embarrassment will soon turn to boredom and you may not be asked again. Go along, smile and join in.

Little by little, enjoyment will replace the anguish of going alone and when you actually ask someone to come for a meal, you will know that another hurdle is over and you are beginning to find your feet again. It will take courage to return alone to an empty house or sleeping children, and no one to talk over the evening with. But we have to make the choice—either to face the world on its own terms or become a forgotten recluse.

If you are fifty-five or older and have not previously been a part of your neighborhood's senior citizens' group, you might want to give it a try. There you are sure to find others who have lost their partners and understand your grief.

A SIMPLE MEAL

I have heard many widows explain that they can no longer have friends round now that there is no man to take his share in the conversation. I suspect that is an excuse rather than a reason! As a first step, why not ask someone who has been a particular help to you to come and share your main meal? You need not put on anything special. Children love to help in the preparations and to be allowed to take part, at least for the first

half-hour, and benefit from being considered adult enough to do so.

Try to do things a little differently from when you entertained as a couple—it will help you to begin your new way of life. Go and browse round the bookshops and you will be sure to find an interesting recipe book. Try a new dish you have not made before. There are plenty of simple cookery books available which show you how to make a tasty, attractive meal.

COURAGE TO CONTINUE

Supporting hands abound for the first few months, but you can't expect to be carried on other people's shoulders for ever. The temptation then is to let yourself go—not to bother with cooking yourself a meal, not to care how you look, taking less interest in things outside your own small world. The fight is on against self-centeredness. You have to make another effort—but the self-discipline involved in taking a pride in yourself even with no one else to notice, brings its own reward of self-respect and confidence.

Christians do not have a monopoly of courage and inner resources. Trust in the goodness of God and in his guiding hand in life obviously provides a security, but there are countless men and women who face bereavement, adjust to it, cope with it and make something good and worthwhile out of it with little or no spiritual support.

BAD PATCHES

From time to time, something happens or is said, usually out of the blue, which reopens the old wounds and tears us apart again. One widow told of a morning when the sun was shining, the children were doing well at school and she herself felt that day able to cope with anything. She turned on the radio and heard a voice describing the place where she and her husband had spent their honeymoon. Desolation overcame her and she sat and wept.

Months—even years—later, such dark times come and remind us how fragile is our resilience. If we need help, it is only sensible to ask for it. Don't be ashamed of yourself—admit how you feel. An understanding friend or a good neighbor will usually be available to encourage you until the cloud lifts.

A NEW VIEWPOINT

Christians often feel guilty when they are depressed. We feel that because faith upheld us at the time of acute crisis, it will automatically go on doing so. But times change and we change; we begin to ask questions which did not occur to us then; faith may waver.

This is when we need to be humble enough to recognize our need of someone else's opinion or assurance and to go to someone we can trust to help us. It is possible to rely too much on our own resources of prayer and our own reading of the Bible. It is tempting to read what we want to believe into a section of the Bible or to pray too self-centeredly. Then, a different view may be all we need to set us on our way again. Our faith may have wavered, but God remains faithful.

KEEPING WELL

A doctor once said that bereavement was like having a surgical operation without an anaesthetic. You will feel very tired, but this is not to say that you must sit down and rest all day. By all means rest whenever you feel a real need to do so, but remember that exercise is also necessary.

A brisk walk each day will give you fresh air and the chance to meet other people for a casual chat. Physical exercise will make you healthily tired so that you sleep better, and will also keep your muscles in trim. Fear and anxiety cause adrenalin to be pumped into the system, making muscles tense.

Adrenalin supplies the energy for bodily activity, so if we don't use our muscles or take enough exercise, it does not get used up. This sets up more tension and frustration.

A BROKEN HEART

Some people fear they will die of a 'broken heart'. This image arises from ancient beliefs that the heart was the chief seat of the emotions. But we must not take this idea literally.

Occasionally, the surviving partner of a marriage may suffer some form of heart disease, but it has not been proved that grief alone is the cause. There are nearly always contributory factors. Understandable though it may be for the distressed person to turn to alcohol, tobacco or pills to dull the ache, the dangers are well-known and a growing dependence on any of them will do harm.

'I CAN'T SLEEP'

Most bereaved people say how they dread sleepless nights of tossing and turning, reliving the past and worrying about the future. Commonly the pattern of sleep is so disturbed that the morning brings a headache as bad as the heartache. Many fear

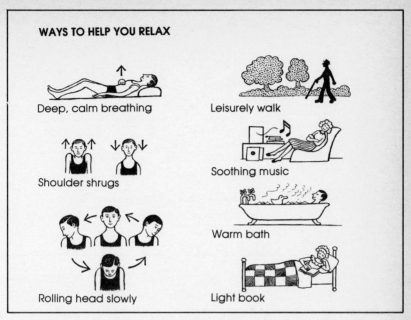

WAYS TO HELP YOU RELAX

Deep, calm breathing

Leisurely walk

Shoulder shrugs

Soothing music

Rolling head slowly

Warm bath

Light book

that if they don't get enough sleep they will be ill. This is not true; given the right conditions—a comfortable bed, warmth, relaxation and tiredness—sleep will eventually come. Don't worry about not sleeping—that is enough on its own to keep sleep away.

Fortunately, there are several things you can do. First, see your doctor. If he thinks it necessary, he will prescribe a short course of sleeping pills to break the pattern of sleepless nights. Then being active during the day will encourage natural sleep. A warm bath followed by a warm drink helps you to relax. Have a tin of crackers by the bed—you won't sleep if you're hungry.

Make sure you are warm. Bed is a cold place when you have been used to another's warmth, and an electric blanket is well worth having.

READING AND LISTENING

If you like reading in bed, you may find an undemanding book or magazine will divert the mind from its whirl of thoughts. Television is another possibility. So is a transistor radio! I am not suggesting that everyone tunes in to loud pop music or stimulating phone-in programs—these would probably send sleep fleeing for some. The sound of a friendly, and quickly familiar, radio voice can be a comfort, and it may soothe you to sleep.

When all else fails, remind yourself that not being able to sleep is not medically harmful. So lie quietly and relaxed; put away the worries of yesterday and anxiety about tomorrow.

And take advantage of the uninterrupted quiet. There is time to remember the good things and be thankful for what remains. A sleepless night can be the opportunity to commit yourself into God's loving hands, expecting the peace he has promised to all who ask for it. The strength to do what we have to comes only when it is needed—not before. God's help is always given at the right time.

A PROPER DIET

Strong emotion often takes away the desire for food. It is common for the bereaved person to feel 'full up', even nauseated at the thought of food. Some, even though they feel hungry, will make do with insufficient food because the effort to cook a meal is too great.

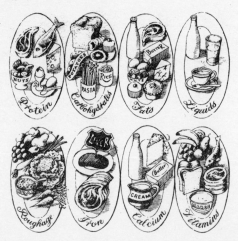

A healthy diet should include every day something from each of the types of food shown above. Proteins, fats and carbohydrates supply the energy we need.

But, however little you feel like cooking or eating, it is essential (as when recovering from illness) to get your strength back and live sensibly. It is foolish to risk being a worry to other people or becoming dependent on them to do something you can do for yourself. Large meals are not called for; it is better to have nutritious foods, little and often.

PSYCHOLOGICAL HELPS

When you are low, it seems impossible to 'think happy'. Yet attitudes of mind *do* influence bodily well-being, so it is a good idea to expect something good to happen each day. From there you may be able to plan to make it happen. This is one way towards restoring self-confidence.

Self-respect may be at a low ebb, too, so it is important to keep up your past standards. Tempting though it may be to slop around the house untidily, it pays to make an effort and dress properly. To see you looking good will make those around you feel that you consider them worth making this effort for. Widowers, too, benefit from keeping a smart appearance, even if it now means learning how to iron. Something new to wear, or a record, book or toy, can cheer up a bereaved child.

HOW THE CHURCH CAN HELP

Don't hesitate about going to church at a time of crisis—even if you have never been before. Ignore the mutterings of bad neighbors. To be welcoming is one of the functions of the church—to be a refuge for those who suffer, and to help any who feel the need to find out what God has to say to them at this low point in their life.

A FULLER LIFE

Many find their loneliness lessened by joining a church group. They find that churches are, by and large, friendly and ready to help. Nearly all churches have neighborhood schemes by which they come to hear of people in special need. By taking advantage of what the church offers socially, widows and widowers and their families can be drawn into activities which they will enjoy and look forward to. Some may find they want to attend a service and, against all expectation, discover the beginning of a fuller life, spiritually as well as socially. Every town and village will have a church and no one need hesitate to take a step in its direction.

IN YOUR OWN TIME

One of the hardest things for some bereaved Christians is to get back into the life of the church. When the whole family once sat, Sunday by Sunday, taking part in the familiar service, going to church may be hard to bear for the person or people left behind.

As always, the sooner we can pick up the threads the easier it will be, but if the bereaved family feels unable to join in Sunday worship for a time, they should not feel guilty about it. The church shouldn't expect too much too soon. The church members can show the warmth of their caring in practical ways, giving sympathy and loving comfort, assuring the family of their prayers on their behalf—and no one who has not experienced this can appreciate fully the strength God gives in answer to other people's prayers.

EMOTIONAL PROBLEMS

LONELINESS

After the death of a husband or wife, we gradually turn to others for company. This is right—what is self-defeating is if we become so dependent on having people with us that we can't bear being alone. We all need some solitude in order to sort ourselves out. It will largely be up to us to arrange our lives so that these times of being alone are balanced by time spent with other people.

REMINDERS

Just as the setting up of a 'shrine' to the dead person only makes the pain last longer, so it is only common sense to avoid the things you know are likely to upset you—an old photograph, a place which had a special meaning for you both. Some people, though, are comforted by photographs: one man I know had framed every picture of his wife he could find.

But another friend put away everything which would

remind her of her dead son. In time, as her anguish lessened, she put up one or two photographs and found they did help her. Do whatever helps you, always realizing that life has to go on and that the past mustn't smother the future.

OUR OWN LIFE

It becomes all too easy to live life through other people—watching television, reading the paper. It is *our* life we have to live. If we want friends who will relive our loneliness, we have to be friendly ourselves; to benefit from others' efforts we have to make an effort ourselves. It is tiring but it is the worthwhile price to pay for getting back into the world. The worst thing the lonely person can do is to sit at home and feel sorry for himself.

If you can, go out at least once a day and if possible at about the same time. People are creatures of habit—it will be easier to smile at someone you meet regularly, and soon you will be on speaking terms.

A WIDER HORIZON

It is surprising but true that there seems no need for anyone to be physically lonely. Everywhere there are clubs and organizations for the lonely. Joining a group of people with similar interests will do the whole family good. The bereaved person with a family can become bogged down with child-minding and keeping the home together, so it is important that the horizons should be widened. For many people these clubs have provided just what they needed: practical help and moral support.

At the same time, they recognize the dangers of catering for only one type of person, the danger of serving more to emphasize the loneliness and separation than to lessen it. And so they all aim at enabling their members gradually to wean themselves away as they feel able.

Information about clubs and organizations can be found in your local library, newspaper or information bureau.

SHARING YOUR HOME

If the prospect of living alone is unbearable, you may consider setting up house with a friend or relative. This arrangement can be highly successful or quite disastrous. The saying, 'You never really know a person until you live with them', is very true. Ensure that you will be able to get on together before committing yourself. Take time to talk about your interests, families, likes and dislikes. Bear in mind that you may both find it difficult to adapt.

When you have decided on a person you think suitable, it may help if you agree that the first fortnight will be a trial period, if circumstances make this possible. At the end of that time you'll know how you get along together.

FAIR DEAL

A shared home usually means that one of you will have to give up most of his own furniture and goods, and may always feel hard done by. Discuss this honestly beforehand.

Certain questions will have to be asked:

- How are the financial arrangements to work?
- Will you live separate lives or do most things together?
- Having decided what you want, can you see the other person being willing to co-operate on those terms?
- How far are **you** willing to give way?

When you are thinking of any kind of sharing, it is wise to have a proper agreement drawn up so that each person knows exactly what is expected. Fix a fair rent for the area if appropriate; and agree a method of splitting gas, electricity and phone bills and household expenses. This sounds cold-blooded, but it will save much argument if difficulties should arise later on.

SEXUAL DEPRIVATION

An aspect of bereavement not often enough acknowledged is sexual deprivation. Whatever one may sometimes be told, it is impossible completely to direct one's sexuality into other channels. Death snatches away the deepest human expression of love, leaving an emptiness which nothing else can fill. The sudden cutting-off of the sex life of a widow or widower sets up

deep tensions. What to do with one's sex drive is a very real problem.

Sexual deprivation adds to loneliness. One widow said that what she missed most after her husband's death was being touched. Bed is a cold place for the bereaved wife or husband. It is not only the sexual acts themselves which are missed, it's the little things—a caress in passing, the joke which no one else sees. To see other people enjoying these can be a painful reminder that you have lost part of yourself.

CASUAL RELATIONSHIPS

Men and women need each other; we all need to hold and be held. Yet to take up some casual sexual relationship is not the answer. Without the depth and commitment of marriage, such an affair is always second-best.

The longing to love and be loved is in no way wrong in itself. But in this situation, as Cardinal Basil Hume has written, 'It is not right to allow other people to fall in love with us . . . if we are silly (and vanity can be the danger here) we may cause pain and hurt, and that is wrong.' For some, masturbation may bring temporary physical release, but the basic need to give oneself to another will not be met and the deprivation may even be intensified.

RESPONSIBLE INVOLVEMENT

This is an area where the Christian is hard hit. Magazines and television all insist that frequent sex is necessary for all, and no concern of anyone except the individuals involved. But Christians believe that the act of sex is the total involvement of one person with another, a complete self-giving. Sex is never an isolated act. There are social as well as personal implications to be considered. Sexual satisfaction is not to be an irresponsible indulgence. Christians believe that sex is a gift from God to be enjoyed but not selfishly exploited.

To be deprived of one's sex-life need not be fatal! At the time when I was quite sure it would be, I read some perceptive words by a young widow: 'While the human organism can get along without physical love-making, it cannot thrive without human affection.' What the bereaved need most is warm concern and continuing love and tenderness.

REMARRIAGE

At the time of bereavement the idea of marrying again will be unthinkable, but people do remarry—a high proportion of widowers do so within five years of losing their wives. A second marriage should be seen as a compliment to the previous partner: never think of it as in any way disloyal. Every relationship is unique. No one need condemn himself to a bleak lifetime of living on past memories and loyalties.

Even so, many do feel a sense of betrayal when contemplating a second marriage. Before entering into a new relationship it is essential to say goodbye to the old one—not forgetting it, but letting it go, never allowing it to come between you and your new life.

A second marriage calls for courage, commitment and a degree of tolerance which can be demanding. But, given the essential ingredients of love and understanding, making it work can bring a deep sense of achievement and fulfilment.

REALISTIC EXPECTATIONS

Bereavement weakens one's self-confidence and the longing for support is sometimes overwhelming, especially when there are young children to bring up alone. The prospect of someone to share the responsibility can be very attractive. For a man, the thought of supporting a new wife and stepchildren, as well as any children he may have himself, can be daunting. But, delicate though the situation may be, the adjustments need not be too much to cope with.

Much of the tension which may arise early in a second marriage comes from fear that you may not live up to the ideals of your new spouse. But you are both as you are—there is no need to compare the new relationship with the old. It should be seen as a new beginning in both your lives. If a first marriage was happy, a second is likely to be so, too. Past experience will have shown that allowances have to be made all round, and any wisdom you gained from your first partnership can be brought to bear on the second.

STEPCHILDREN

By the time of your second marriage, the children will already be getting to know their new step-parent quite well, and they will be happy for you. But if they are younger they may guard your love for them jealously, not wanting to have to share you with someone else. In this situation, you will need to show them that you still love them just as much.

If your new partner also has children, it may help, if you can afford it, to start afresh in a new home. This avoids the problem of children resenting the intrusion of others into what has been their territory until now. In any case, you are going to have to encourage a great deal of giving and sharing.

Discipline is a tricky subject, and you may find that your new partner has different views from your own. You are both now responsible for both sets of children, so it is important to follow an agreed, consistent course.

WHERE TO LIVE—AND HOW

All sorts of practical problems arise almost at once when you have lost your husband or wife. Fortunately, most questions can be left for a while until you are better able to deal with them.

DECISIONS, DECISIONS

Don't do anything in a hurry. If it is at all possible, major decisions should be postponed for at least six months. At first, judgment is unlikely to be reliable and it will be difficult to see things clearly. A line of action which seems best at the time may prove a mistake.

Never be afraid to ask for advice and opinion on those matters which you don't know about. Most people are more than willing to make suggestions. Not all of these will be equally helpful, but accept them in the spirit in which they are given, weigh up all the arguments and keep them in your mind until you feel able to come to a sensible decision. Business friends or workmates will be able to help in their own fields, neighbors will come and help in the house, and your priest or minister will want to share with you Christian comfort and strength.

HOW SHALL WE MANAGE?

Nearly all bereaved families find themselves worse off financially, so the first problem to solve is how to manage with the money available. This is true even when it is the wife who has died, because the husband may have to arrange for any children to be looked after. If there are no relatives or friends who can look after the children, the father may have to arrange for paid help in the home, which can be very expensive indeed. These considerations are good reasons for families to take out life insurance policies on homemakers. Work-at-home wives may not be contributing to the family income, but their absence will add strain to any budget. (See also section headed 'The one-parent family'.)

A BASIC YEAR'S BUDGET

As soon as you know how much money will be available for living expenses, it helps to draw up a simple budget, at least for the first year. A widow will probably need to supplement her pension and insurance, especially if she has children to support. She may know already how much she needs to cover food, clothing, school expenses and so on, but may have little knowledge of how much she will need for rent, heating, telephone, licenses, insurance and all the big bills which come when she is least prepared to deal with them. These can add up to an alarming amount, and a detailed list of what they are and when they fall due will make it easier to see where cut-backs have to be made.

Once your financial position is clear, it is worth asking the social services department whether you are eligible for food stamps or extra help.

MAKING ECONOMIES

Although it is important not to cut back on items like proper food, it is often easy to make substantial savings, particularly by re-organizing your largest expenses. If you run a car, you may decide that you could make do with public transport. You may be able to take vacations out of peak season. It may be possible to save by adjusting heaters so that rooms are kept at a lower temperature when not in use. Proper insulation in the attic and insulating the hot-water tank will also cut fuel costs fast.

WHERE TO LIVE—AND HOW / 67

WHERE SHALL WE LIVE?

A common reaction to bereavement is the feeling that you must move right away to a new area where no one knows you and you can start again. More common still is the desire to move house in order to be near a relative, friend or married child.

A CAREFUL DECISION

But this decision should not be taken without a great deal of thought. Over and over again, one hears of a hurried move to a strange part of the country where the bereaved person no longer has the comfort of familiar landmarks and finds that few people are interested in his/her troubles.

One elderly widower could not bear to go on living in the old home after his wife died, so against all advice he sold up and bought a house in the same town as his married daughter. Soon after, his son-in-law was sent abroad for two years and the old man had no one of his own to visit or talk to. He became more and more of a recluse, and before the two years were up, he too had died.

Of course, it can be a good idea to move. The important thing to remember is that this step should only be taken when you are sure you are no longer dependent on your present neighbors and environment. For parents, the decision to move will probably be made when the last child leaves home. For others, the decision may come when friends retire and move away. By then, you will be able to see more clearly what you want to do and where you want to be.

Some widows have no choice but to give up their homes; lack of money forces it on them and they have to look around for a smaller house which will be cheaper to run. If housing is a problem, call the housing office of your local county or city government and see if you qualify for their assistance. *Turning Home Equity into Income for Older Americans* is available for $3.00 from Consumer Information Center, Department L, Pueblo, Colo, 81009.

RESTLESSNESS

Acute restlessness is common in bereavement. This may take the form of frequent visits to people around the country. Friends and relatives will not like to say 'No' when you invite yourself for a day or two, but hectic travel is best avoided or at least postponed. Other people are usually leading busy lives and your self-absorption and possibly somewhat irrational behavior will not make you a wholly welcome guest.

The wife of someone I knew was widowed while she and her husband were on vacation. The chain of events following her bereavement presents a classic example of bad advice. She sold the house from a distance because she could not bear the thought of coming back; she moved round the country from married child to married child; she stayed two or three nights with various friends in turn, living out of her suitcase for months on end.

She never came to terms with what had happened, was bereft of old friends in her own neighborhood, at the mercy of realtors and quack medical opinions, and prey to every fear that a vivid imagination could produce. In the end she bought a cottage in a remote village where she and her husband had once spent a vacation.

You can't run away from your situation. Wherever you go, your grief goes with you. Until you have worked through it, you are better in your own place, among people you know well.

STAYING WHERE YOU ARE

In the same way, it isn't always a good idea to accept kindly-meant offers of hospitality immediately after bereavement. Going away is always easier than coming back. If you feel you must have extra support—either because there will be no one else in the house or because there are young children to cope with—accept an offer from someone sympathetic to come and stay with you for a short time. That way, you will not sit about with nothing to do but think, you will not have to be a 'good guest', and you will be able to do the day-to-day jobs as usual.

Sometimes, to be in someone else's house with little to do and worrying about what needs to be done at home adds to the alarm and frustration. It is better to stick it out and begin to come to terms with the situation, and then, when you feel reasonably confident of being able to return home without too much pain, to spend a short time away with friendly and agreeable people.

By that time, you will be needing a rest and will be able to relax better for knowing that the immediate decisions have been taken and jobs attended to. Being away from it all will then provide a sense of balance and proportion to enable you to look ahead sensibly. When you do go back, it helps immeasurably to have someone with you to stay just long enough to see you settled in.

IF YOU HAVE TO MOVE
It is doubly hard that the problems of finding a new home come at a time when you are least able to cope with it all. Shop slowly. Look long enough to know what is available in your price range and to get a sense of what you need to make you most content. Some people feel they must have grass, others need to feel they are secure, or within walking distance of a shopping area.

LIVING WITH RELATIVES
However tempted and pressurized you may be, consider carefully before agreeing to live with relatives.

Understanding and adaptable though your relatives may be, you and your children will need somewhere of your own where you can work out your problems and attitudes together, free from criticism and unwanted advice.

EARNING A LIVING

PROS AND CONS

After where to live, the most pressing problem will be how to
make enough money to live on. This will be particularly hard for
the young widow with children and also for the young widower
who may have to pay for someone to look after the children.
The young mother will have to decide whether or not to go out
to work. In many cases, she will have to. All the same, there
are pros and cons to be considered.

- Will going out to work mean that your children will have to be
looked after?
- What will you do in school holidays?

FINDING A JOB

Even if you decide that you would be better off working, and
look for a full-time job outside the home, it may be hard to find
exactly what you want.

You need to ask yourself: 'What do I enjoy doing? What am I able to do? What is the effect likely to be on the children? Will it be better to get a job outside the home and have more money, or to stay at home and manage with less? Should I take an outside job so as to help myself, psychologically, and be a more interesting person?'

This can be the time to reassess your personality; it can be an opportunity to receive that peace of mind which is so necessary. To commit the situation to God and to wait patiently for opportunities is the way to a calm mind.

MAKE YOUR HOUSE WORK

If you own your house but may have difficulty in keeping it going, how can the house itself help? Have you, or can you improvise, a spare room? If so, would you be willing to let it? Universities and colleges never seem to have enough rooms for both staff and students.

FINDING A LODGER

The advantage of letting a room to someone connected with education is that you will probably have the vacation free, while still receiving a small retaining fee. Decide whether you would prefer to give someone full board (more of a tie), bed, breakfast and evening meal, bed and breakfast, or accommodation only. Find out whether your lodger will be there at weekends and if so whether the same meals arrangement will apply. Discuss with them whether they wish to share everything with you and your family, or whether their 'freedoms' are limited.

Decide whether you want a man, woman, boy or girl. What sort of age would you prefer—a young student, a slightly older person, a middle-aged person perhaps on a temporary assignment in your area? Another adult or near-adult in the house has definite advantages: it means that someone else will be there in case of household disasters or sudden illness; they can also provide new ideas, a more balanced view of life. The mere fact of someone coming in and out may give that extra sense of security you need. A lodger with whom you get on well can be a help in many ways.

THE LEGAL SIDE

A lawyer will advise you on drawing up a properly worded lease so that your agreement with your tenant is clear and legal and binding.

If you live in rented accommodation, and want to sub-let a room, you may need to ask your landlord for written permission.

When you make your tax return you must include any rent you have received. You can, however, deduct the cost of such expenses as preparing the room, putting right any damage caused, and necessary replacement of furnishings.

SHARED HOUSING

The Shared Housing Resource Center,
6344 Greene St, Philadelphia, Pa. 19144
is a clearing house of information on setting up a housing situation that is mutually beneficial to the home owner and the center. Their prime concern is helping older citizens in need of a place to live or in need of a roomer who will pay or work for his rent. They offer a *Home Sharing Self-Help Guide* ($2.75), a listing of local match-up programs, and other informative publications.

YOUR GARDEN

There are several ways in which even a small garden can bring in a little much-needed money. You could try growing herbs, which take up little room and are much in demand from people wanting to use fresh products rather than dried. Have you fruit trees or bushes? Can you grow tomatoes? Do you have success with a certain type of flower? If space is limited, it is better to concentrate on one product in order to start to build up a local reputation for it, both privately and among the stores.

WORKING OUTSIDE THE HOME

What did you do before you married? Was it something you could take up again without too much effort? Were you, perhaps, a typist, a hairdresser, a schoolteacher or a nurse? Whatever you did for a living, even if you haven't kept your hand in, it is possible to take it up again. There is probably an evening class you could attend for a short session until you are competent once more.

The National Federation of Business and Professional Women's Clubs, 2012 Massachusetts Ave, NW, Washington, DC 20036, has information about student loans for women over 35.

Check with a nearby community college, college or university to see if they offer classes (and loans) that will be of help. Their main campus may be outside of easy commuting distance, but many offer extension classes as part of their continuing education program. Many high schools also offer classes for adults. Learning a new skill may open doors to opportunities you didn't even know existed.

GIVING A SERVICE

Are you good at flower arranging? If so, let people know that you are willing to do the floral decorations for local functions or weddings. An easy way to get your name known is to do your first piece of work for a friend or someone you know in the neighborhood. If it goes well and complimentary comments are made, not only will your confidence be increased, the orders will soon start coming in.

Do you enjoy meeting people and feel you could go round selling cosmetics or other goods to people in their homes? There are often advertisements in the local papers for representatives. The best plan is, first find out what is needed in your own area and then set out to satisfy that need.

CAN YOU DRIVE?

If you have a car it may now prove too expensive to run and maintain, but a car spells freedom and independence. If you work out the cost of fares on public transport for your family, the cost difference may not turn out to be so great. Make enquiries locally and find out if a store or a firm would employ you as a driver, perhaps part-time. What about delivering newspapers? Driving a school bus? Would it be possible to run a private taxi-service? To do this you will, of course, have to fulfil all the legal requirements and be comprehensively covered by your insurance company.

If you plan to run a small business from your home, you will have to consult the local byelaws as you may need a license or zoning clearance. If you are in rented accommodation, you may need the consent of the landlord.

Before setting up in business, it is worth getting advice from:

- your bank manager
- a lawyer
- an accountant
- your local Small Business Administration

EARNING AT HOME

For a parent with still-young children, this is the ideal way of supplementing the family income. It allows flexibility and does not entail the expenses involved in traveling, dressing well, buying food out, and so on.

HOME COOKING

Are you a good cook? Home cooking is always in demand. Again, it would probably be better to concentrate on one thing you know you do well. Your speciality will soon become known and sought after, be it your pastry or your steak-and-kidney pudding.

I know one widow who advertised the fact that she would cook as many quiches as people would order. In three months she had to buy a freezer, to be able to cook in advance for parties and regular orders. In five years she had a chain of stores in four different towns, all turning out her own recipe and expanding all the time. You may not want to do anything on such a scale, but your own local stores may well be interested.

Start by telling a few people what you intend to do; put an advertisement in your local paper. If you feel able to try your hand at private catering, let it be known that you will suggest menus, cater for, cook and deliver food for small parties.

SAFEGUARDS

Any work done at home is open to risk. Setting up business from home may be quite involved and legal advice should

WORK AT HOME

- typing
- baby-sitting
- cake decorating
- embroidery
- dressmaking and alterations

- carpentry or carving
- telephone selling
- music lessons
- preparing taxes

always be obtained before starting. Some local ordinances are very strict on inspection of kitchens where food for sale is prepared. A recent survey shows that many home workers earn a pittance. Before you decide what you would like to do at home, find out the proper rate for the job in your area.

CLOTHING

Other skills much in demand are home dressmaking, crochet and embroidery. If you are good at sewing, you can also earn money by altering clothes, especially children's which are outgrown but not outworn and which need adjustment for the next child.

HELP!

If you feel you might qualify for government assistance, do not hesitate to query your local social services office. You might be eligible for food stamps, subsidy for your child's school lunch, etc.

FURTHER INFORMATION

'555 Ways to Earn Money' by Jay Conrad Levinson (Holt, Reinhart and Winston, NY, NY.)
'You Can Live On Half Your Income' by Camilla Luckey (Zondervan, Grand Rapids, Mich.).

THE BEREAVED CHILD

Sooner or later, a child comes home with the news that a friend's mommy or daddy has died. Our immediate reaction is to say 'How dreadful!'—and change the subject. But the child may be frightened and bewildered, hit by the fact that death happens not only on television but to real people and therefore, perhaps, even his own parents.

TALKING ABOUT DEATH

This is when we should stop whatever we are doing, express our own shock and sorrow and speak naturally about what has happened. Ask if your child thinks there is anything you could do to help. Suggest that he is particularly kind to his friend—he might ask him or her round to play, for example.

This way of dealing with a terrifying situation will do much to reassure the child. It will give him a chance to help his friend practically. It will also give him a sense of security to know that if it ever happened to him, he would be looked after, and that even such a disaster as this can be coped with.

WHEN DEATH COMES

We must never shut children out of a grief the whole family shares. It is impossible completely to protect them from what has happened, but they need not suffer permanent emotional damage.

The most unobtrusive way of teaching children how to cope with death is by helping them to see that from time to time suffering comes into every life, as when the cat brings in a bird it has killed. They will experience it in the death of a dearly-loved pet, or even when a friend moves away. It is at such times that we can reassure the child he is not alone in his sadness and that within the family sorrow is natural.

NEVER TELL LIES

One child was told that her daddy had gone abroad, another that her mommy was in the hospital. Both children eventually heard that their parents had died, and suffered much greater shock, made worse by the permanent distrust they came to feel for all adults and the fear that any separation might mean death.

Honesty is just as essential within a Christian family. The child who said bitterly that God was 'no good' was reacting perfectly rationally to his father's death in a plane crash, for his mother had often said that God would keep him safe. Children soon learn that Christians are not immune to disaster. Always assure them that, for those whose lives are committed to God, whatever happens can be turned to good, and that such experiences should give us greater sympathy for all who suffer.

SOME COMMON FEARS

As well as the shock of unbelief at the death of a parent, a child may be afraid of losing the other as well. He may ask constantly, 'How old are you?' Young children may even think that everyone else in the family is about to die. Imaginative children may be frightened that the parent's ghost will return and haunt them. Bedtime is dreaded and brings on symptoms such as sweating, bed-wetting and nightmares. Some children insist on having the window closed 'in case daddy comes in'.

Younger children may worry that their mommy or daddy

will marry someone else, especially if they have read old-fashioned stories about wicked stepmothers. In such cases, a widowed mother must assure them that the man who drops in to do a household job is simply giving a helping hand, while a father can explain that the woman who brings round a cake is being friendly.

It is important to allow the child to talk about his fears, so that the hidden ones can be brought into the open and dealt with. If the childen withdraw into themselves, we have to watch their reactions carefully. We must be sensitive to try to understand what may be making them anxious.

A CONSTRUCTIVE ATTITUDE

A child's attitude to death will be colored by our own. If we have taught our children compassion for others, they will find it easier to accept bereavement. They will tend to assume that as we have previously helped friends, it is now the turn of those friends to do the same for us! This attitude will help prevent bitterness. But we must never deny what has happened. Refusal to face facts will only raise false hopes, confuse the child and make it more difficult for him to adjust.

FEAR, GUILT AND SHOCK

The effects of bereavement on a child will depend on many things—his age, his own personality and the reactions of the family. When a parent dies, the child feels let down and

abandoned. Was it because he was 'naughty' or disobedient? Guilt and self-doubt build up. He remembers the time he said, 'I wish you were dead', and may believe he has actually killed his mommy or daddy.

Another child may appear to be indifferent or downright callous. Susan was told that her mother had been killed in a car smash. 'Has she?' she said. 'Is lunch ready?' This reaction is due to intense shock and is the child's automatic defence mechanism, so it would be out of place to rebuke her for being flippant or unfeeling.

EXPLAINING DEATH

How much to tell a child about death should always depend on how much he wants to know. This will be discovered by the sort of questions he asks.

Children soon realize that death marks the end of life (though, as Christians believe, the beginning of another) and that death brings sorrow and grief. But children are as resilient as they are vulnerable, and with help and support they can survive almost any experience so long as they are surrounded by love.

The way in which we describe death will depend on our own beliefs, but we have to remember that children are matter-of-fact thinkers. It does nothing to soften the blow if we use such expressions as 'gone to sleep'; 'gone to heaven'; 'passed away'. They may know already that dead things are buried or burned, and they will be able to accept that this is what happens to dead people too, if we do not attempt to gloss over the fact.

ANSWERING THEIR QUESTIONS

When something touches them deeply and personally the questions children ask are among the most difficult for the adult to answer. None of us knows why death comes to someone young or healthy, nor do we know what happens after death has taken place.

I firmly believe that a background of Christian belief does much to comfort a child at this time. We are able to assure him that although we don't know why death has come to his mommy or daddy or to some other member of the family, we do know that the love of God is unshakeable and holds us all, in life and in death, and that nothing can separate us from him.

This, of course, is far too abstract for a grieving child fully to take in, but in our own case I found that it was possible to illustrate this by pointing out that all the kindness, invitations, flowers and letters that we received were God's way of showing us his love—by sending other people to look after us.

THE CHILD'S MOURNING

To mourn is just as much a psychological necessity for the child as for the adult and cannot be rushed. He needs time to be sad, to remember, to work through the feelings of loneliness and loss. It may help him if he talks about his feelings so that he comes to understand what is going on inside him, and so can cope with his emotional conflict.

GOING TO THE FUNERAL

It is natural to wish to spare children the ordeal of the funeral service, but we should think again. To be present and take part in this ritual exorcises many fears and helps the child, like the adult, to face the reality of death. However harrowing the sight of a grieving child may be, he needs to face the truth.

PATTERNS OF BEHAVIOR

Many children react to death with anti-social behavior and aggressiveness, disguising their fear by demanding that everything should be all right again. The bereaved child may be hostile to other members of the family; he may be 'rude' or unnaturally noisy.

Generally speaking, children under the age of five appear to ignore the fact of death because it is beyond their understanding, though they will be well aware of the atmosphere of distress in the home and will respond with various anxiety symptoms, often becoming demanding and clinging.

Between the ages of five and nine, they think of death as a punishment on them for their naughtiness and that, if they are 'good', the dead person will come back again—this is why it is important for this age group to attend the funeral and be helped to realize death's finality. It is not until they are ten or eleven that children understand death more fully.

Following the first shock and tears, there often follows a period of quiet despair. The child may become withdrawn and unable to concentrate on anything. As a result, his school work will suffer. He needs reassurance that this is perfectly normal and is nature's way of giving him a rest until he is strong enough to take the strain. We have to judge when the time has come to nudge him out of himself once more.

HELPING THE CHILD RECOVER

By talking to the children and giving them plenty of time to talk to us, we help each other. In times of grief, habit is a great help and children should go to school as usual and be encouraged to do jobs about the house. This will give them a renewed sense of purpose.

Schools can play a vital part. In these days, there will almost certainly be several other children at school with only one parent. Although insensitive and cruel in other ways, children treat a bereaved friend much more kindly and naturally than the adult world treats the bereaved parent. In my experience, teachers, too, go out of their way to support the child, and should always be told what has happened, especially if exams are looming.

OUTSIDE HELP

Although the family should not shut itself away, we should be wary about accepting invitations on the children's behalf too soon after the death. Balance is essential—at first, we shall all be tempted to stay indoors in miserable isolation. Many teenagers, however, will feel that their entire social life has been cut off. It is important for them to emerge as soon as they feel able to cope with the inevitable curious looks and attempts to take their minds off it.

With younger children it can be counter-productive to push them out against their will. We must decide carefully whether they need protecting a little longer or whether they should be given a gentle push. One solution is to encourage their friends into your home. This will also be good for you: it will now be more necessary than ever to keep up with youthful attitudes and ideas to bring up a family single-handed.

THE ONE-PARENT FAMILY

ADAPTATION

Bringing up children single-handed is hard work and there is no
virtue in trying to be independent and going it alone. People are
willing to lend a hand, and organizations exist to help and
advise. Many men will be glad to take fatherless boys to a
football match, or even on holiday with their own family.
Neighbors and friends will sometimes offer to take children
shopping, or to a show or concert. It is both rude and foolish to
refuse such kindness.

PARENTS' ROLES

It very quickly becomes obvious that it is impossible for anyone
to be both mother and father. Losing a parent means that the
family is incomplete and all its members have to learn to live
within the new limitations. However, I tried to take an intelligent
interest in my sons' passions. I began to watch televised football
with them and found I was becoming interested myself.

Children have an innate sense of fair play and the boys co-operated by entering into my hobbies, offering advice on knitting patterns or designs—and always ready with food suggestions!

WHERE TO GO FOR HELP

Not every single-parent family is surrounded by good friends and neighbors. Not all bereaved adults are able to cope. The parent often feels isolated and alone with his problems, but several organizations exist to give advice and practical help. (See names and addresses given in section headed 'What will it mean?')

Big Brothers and Big Sisters of America, 117 South 17th St, Suite 1200, Philadelphia, Pa., 19103, offers emotional help to any fatherless boy or motherless girl. Contact their national headquarters for information about a local program.

LOOKING FORWARD

Sometimes the parent will involve the children in a family decision, to raise their drooping self-confidence. But as they grow up, they may turn to others outside the family to discuss

some problem they would rather not talk about to us.

We must not resent this; our main concern is that they grow up wisely, no matter who helps them do so. Our task is to supply the security they need to enter into the full life which is their birthright as children of God. There must never be pressure on a child to stay at home to keep mother or father company. We bring up children solely to equip them to leave us, free and independent.

REMARRIAGE

Freedom is also *our* right—we may remarry, and if we have taught our children respect for individual freedom, they will understand. Provided that we and our children have 'let go' of the dead parent, this new relationship can be welcomed and entered into with hope. Reassure the children that to remarry is not disloyal to the previous partner, nor does it mean that they have been forgotten.

CLOSER FAMILY LIFE

Any study of one-parent families is bound to be depressing. But most families do survive—not unmarked, but with scars that heal. Families with a forward-looking approach and a faith to carry them along have the best chance.

Bereavement can result in closer family intimacy. Discipline can be simpler when there is only one parent, and in the new atmosphere of mutual concern you can explain why certain things are not allowed. The generation gap can be bridged: when you have seen each other with defenses down and deep feelings expressed, such difficult subjects as sex, politics and religion become easier to discuss.

NEW ACHIEVEMENTS

In a newspaper article, a lone father put his own hopeful views. He said, 'The one-parent family only survives if it pulls together. I used to tell my daughters, "Put into it as much as you take out."' He got to know his children thoroughly. He felt a sense of achievement in looking after each child properly. It gave an extra dimension to his life. He thinks his daughters also benefited, later on, when they had to make their own decisions.

HOW CAN OTHERS HELP?

After a death, everyone wants to help but doesn't know how to. It isn't easy to know, because the persons bereaved will usually be unable to decide what they want. They need time to take in what has happened, and in the meantime practical help.

Unless there has been a definite request for 'no letters', a note of sympathy can bring a warm touch of comfort. It should be brief and should not refer to any other matter. Don't worry about what to say—provided you write from the heart, you will strike the right note. This is no time to be formal. Here is an example of the sort of letter you could send:

> My dear Paul,
>
> We have just heard the sad news. I know you have your family with you, but if there is anything we can do to help, you know you have only to ask.
>
> Words are little help at a time like this and so I won't burden you with a long letter, but simply assure you that we are thinking of you and praying that God will comfort and strengthen you all in these sad days.
>
> With our deepest sympathy and our love,
>
> Mary and John

HELP FROM THE FAMILY

The family is the obvious source of help, but not all families are dependable. Some people will have no family at all, and many other families are widely scattered. Nevertheless, however seldom they meet and whatever the tensions between them, at the time of bereavement they can be a source of great comfort and solidarity in the face of an uncertain future. As a widow said, 'I hadn't seen half of them for years but somehow it felt we were all close because we'd all lost one of the family.'

HELP FROM ORGANIZATIONS

Many organizations have been set up to help the bereaved. Such clubs must be seen not as ends in themselves, but as stepping-stones between one stage of life and another. Otherwise, the danger is that they will become inward-looking and their members may feed on each other's fears and depressions instead of overcoming them. The organizations themselves recommend that their members leave once they feel strong enough. But in the early months many people are relieved to discover that they are not alone.

PROFESSIONAL HELP

As well as family, friends and neighbors, there are also those whose 'jobs' bring them into contact with the bereaved, and who are there to give their professional help.

THE CHURCH

One of the first visitors to the bereaved family is likely to be a clergyman. Ministers say that this is a side of their work in which they feel most at a loss. The minister should not be disconcerted if the bereaved's faith seems shaken; it may be that he or she is having to ask questions for the first time. Nearly all the people I have spoken to agree that the clergyman who gave them most help was the one who recognized that there was nothing he could say to alter the fact of death, but who in some way conveyed that they were not alone in their suffering.

On the other hand, the church *has* got something to say. A woman was grieving inconsolably for her husband, killed by a tractor. When the pastor came, she only said, 'Go away, you can't help me.' He put his hand on her head. 'I *can* help you,' he told her. 'I am here on God's behalf. I have his authority to bring you comfort and peace.'

MEDICAL HELP

Most people, however, now turn more naturally to the medical profession than to the church. Seventy-five per cent of bereaved people visit their doctor during the first six months after the death. Regrettably, only a few minutes can be allotted to each patient these days. But time is just what the bereaved person needs—he cannot marshal his thoughts to describe his symptoms and feelings adequately in five minutes.

The doctor, however, is often forced into prescribing sleeping pills and tranquilizers, without the advice that should go with them. These drugs have their place, but more important by far is the listening ear, reassurance, and a promise that they can come to the office whenever they need to.

Doctors also have to understand why angry words may be hurled at them—this is the urge of the bereaved to rationalize death and to find a scapegoat. The bereaved person needs confidence in the doctor to understand grief and its effects. Here, the doctor can help by pointing out that sometimes life is tragic, there are some things that can't be drugged away.

Health visitors and social workers who see bereaved people can help a great deal in providing moral support. They can tell a young widow it is natural that she finds the children difficult to cope with, while watching for any sign that the pressures are becoming too great. They can, above all, listen objectively, give a problem its own proportion, and give advice from their considerable experience.

HOW FRIENDS CAN HELP

Try not to shower the bereaved man or woman with too much advice. Plans will have to be made, but the value of reliable, trustworthy friends lies in their willingness to listen, reassure and encourage. Add a little congratulation on the progress being made—this does much to raise spirits!

Pity is not helpful—it only leads to self-pity. What is needed is understanding compassion backed up by practical help. Keeping a home running smoothly, cooking meals, doing the laundry are huge burdens to an exhausted father or mother. Spontaneous and thoughtful acts of kindness will be much appreciated—a cake, an offer to take the children to the park, an invitation for Sunday lunch. For six Sundays running after

my husband died, a good friend had us all to lunch and then allowed me to sleep all afternoon while her husband took the children out. It was those Sundays that kept us all sane!

VISITING

Frequent short visits are more valuable than occasional long ones. They are a reminder that you are not forgotten. Visitors often find conversation difficult. This is understandable, because talking about things that must now appear trivial will seem wrong, and this rules out large areas of normal chat. As it is impossible to ignore what has happened, it is better to say right at the start how sorry you are.

There can be no 'right' thing to say—the only way is to speak openly and warmly and take your cue from the other person's reaction. The same approach is needed when speaking to the children—this is a time when they must be treated like adults, with dignity.

Be prepared for anything, from laughter to tears. A friend can be just the person to confide in when members of the family may be too upset. You may be playing a most important part in the bereaved person's recovery.

LONG-TERM CARING

Encourage them to pick up threads as soon as possible. Try to include them in normal activities—not just when you haven't anything better to do. And not only in the first few, dreadful weeks, but to go on caring, visiting and making the effort to see behind the answer 'Oh, I'm fine', when you ask them how they are. Months, even years, later there will be bad patches which can be worse than the first effects of grief. By sympathetically drawing them out you may be helping them over another hump.

It is important for friends not to be too forceful when giving their opinions; the bereaved person has little enough self-confidence and your apparently impregnable position will only injure it still more. Most people, given the chance to speak aloud about a problem, find it working itself out in their minds while they talk. Gentle encouragement and the suggestion of some side of it which may not have occurred to them may be all that is necessary.

Never try to force anyone to reveal their deepest feelings unless they want to—some are too personal or distressing. We have to distinguish between pity, which serves only to feed self-pity, and true comfort which strengthens. Genuine concern is what counts, plus the attempt to put yourself in their place: avoid the trite clichés which would drive you mad if they were said to you.

SELF-RESPECT

The aim of all those wanting to help the bereaved should be to raise their dignity, self-respect and self-dependence. If there are very young children, an offer to baby-sit will be appreciated as most young widows cannot afford to pay and so find themselves spending every evening at home. A vague 'Let me know if I can do something' is rarely anything more than conventional politeness. It's best to decide on something which they will need help with—the washing, cooking or shopping—and offer to do that.

If the bereaved person has to ask for help on too many

levels, it will only add to the general sense of inadequacy. A widow is usually reluctant to ask a friend's husband for help, fearing that his wife may suspect her motives. And make it sound as though you'd like to do the job—almost as though the bereaved person would be doing you a favor by allowing you to do it!

I remember having a dreadful cold and sitting looking at a basket overflowing with damp clothes when a friend dropped in, took everything in at a glance and said, 'Oh, do let me do that ironing while we talk—I can't bear washing but I love ironing and I'd really enjoy it.' She was so convincing I still don't know whether it was true or not, but I was grateful!

Occasions like school prizegivings or sports days can bring acute anguish for the lone parent, not only because of the array of husbands and wives together but because you wish the children's father or mother could see them now. The support of another person close to the family can make all the difference. The children will be pleased that they are worth coming to see and the parent will not feel so much the odd one out.

COMMON FEARS

Many people, especially women, may be frightened of going into an empty house after dark—or even in the daytime. If you have taken a friend home after a trip to the stores or an evening out, it really is a kindness to insist on going at least as far as the hall with them. There is nothing so forlorn as a silent, empty house and it is a relief to be helped over those first few minutes.

PREPARING FOR BEREAVEMENT

I shall always be glad that my husband and I once discussed the inevitable fact that one of us would die before the other. Medical evidence shows that being prepared does help the bereaved person, and lessens the confusion which follows any death. Apart from the advantage of knowing where to turn for help, there will be the comfort of knowing what you decided together.

MAKING A WILL

Both husband and wife should make a will even if there seems little of value to leave. Otherwise, when his wife dies, the husband won't know what she wanted to be done with her goods—and there will be needless legal problems.

Engage a lawyer to draw up the will; this isn't very expensive. You simply make an appointment and take with you:

- a list of your savings and belongings, with their value
- the names of two people who have agreed to act as executors (i.e. to distribute the belongings after your death)
- the names of the people you want to inherit your property, whether specific items or a proportion

The lawyer prepares the will, which you then sign with witnesses present (they mustn't benefit under the will). It is best to let the lawyer keep the will safe, and for you to keep a copy at home with the lawyer's address.

CHILDREN

Remember to make provision for any children, financially and for their upbringing. There is a possibility, however small, that the parents may both be killed, and so the will should say who is to be responsible for the children. You will need to get the people you choose as guardians to agree, of course. When considering who they should be, the interest of the children must come first. Some children worry about the possibility of their parents' dying; if they ask 'What will happen to us if you both die?' they can be reassured to know that Peter and Mary Brown, whom they know and trust, will look after them.

SORTING OUT YOUR AFFAIRS

YOUR HOUSE

If you are buying your house, make sure that your life insurance is linked to the mortgage—it is essential to know that you will still have a roof over your head if your partner dies. If the house is already your own, discuss whether one partner can afford to live in it without the other. If you rent your home, is the lease in the husband's name only? If so, the wife may be given notice to leave.

MONEY AND DOCUMENTS

Remember that it will be impossible to get any money under the terms of the will until the legal formalities have been completed. Try to ensure that somewhere (e.g. a joint bank account) there is a sum of money, however small, which the bereaved partner can call on to tide over the immediate demands.

DO YOU KNOW WHERE THEY ARE?

- husband's will
- wife's will
- insurance policies
- bank passbooks
- mortgage agreement or lease
- birth certificates
- marriage certificates
- Social Security Cards
- Military discharge papers
- Most recent income tax return
- bonds or stock certificates
- car registration and proof of insurance
- land deeds
- check book
- automobile title
- credit cards
- driving licenses

In times of stress, we do not think clearly and memories are faulty, so make sure you both know where all the important documents are kept which may have to be produced. You don't need to understand everything involved, but to have a grasp of the basics will make all the difference.

FUNERAL ARRANGEMENTS

Many people like to know exactly where they will be buried and what kind of service they will have. This puts their mind at ease and makes decisions easier for those left behind.

Your family might consider joining a memorial society, a consumer group which helps its members by providing information about the most reasonably costing funeral and disposal services available in local areas. Memberships in memorial societies are inexpensive. For local information contact: Continental Association of Funeral and Memorial Societies, 1146 19th St NW, Washington, DC, 20036.

ORGAN DONATION

More and more people are choosing to donate some of their usable organs to further the cause of life. If you wish to do this, you must give written permission before your death. Uniform donor cards are, in some states, part of a driver's application. Cards are also available from: American Medical Association, 535 N. Dearborn St, Chicago, Ill. 60610.

COPING WITH SERIOUS ILLNESS

Sometimes death strikes without warning but more often there is a period of illness first. Although this is a harrowing time, it can be used in some degree to prepare the family for bereavement if it should come.

Life has changed; it has narrowed to visits to the hospital, long hours at the bedside. There is the feeling of panic and of resentment. Severe illness is an emotional drain for everyone, and it helps to recognize this and to adjust to living from one day to the next.

For Christians, it should be easier to discuss openly what is happening. If the sick person is still mentally aware, it can be a source of comfort to face the future together, drawing on the promises of God that life goes on after death and that his loving protection will embrace those left behind.

HANDLING THE SITUATION

However feeble the patient may be, treat him normally, not like a baby. Try to understand his needs—if he wants to talk, let him; if he wants you to talk, do so calmly and normally.

Organize things so that at some period each day you can be by yourself to regain your sense of proportion. Don't be too hard on yourself—you won't be able to keep it up.

RELATIONSHIPS

Another way to prepare for bereavement is to lead a full and friendly life. It is never good for a couple to be too self-sufficient and dependent on each other to the exclusion of other people. Old friendships should be kept up and new ones formed all the way through life. Then the loneliness of bereavement will be lessened by the care and concern of all sorts of people.

Children who are brought up in a home where people are always coming and going learn to be outgoing and friendly and to benefit from different outlooks and relationships.

SHARING THE WORK

Equality between the sexes means that the traditional roles of men and women are changing. These days, either may do the other's traditional work. So men should know how to use the washing-machine and change a diaper. Women should learn how to cope with minor electrical faults, decorate a room, etc.

Teach the children any jobs within their scope. Boys usually enjoy cooking and will find life much easier later on if they can sew on a button and press their jeans. It is to everyone's advantage if all the members of the family are taught how to drive the car, and so on.

OTHER WORK INTERESTS

As the children grow up, it is a good thing for wives to think over the practical and psychological advantages of brushing up their pre-marriage jobs or taking further training of some sort, in anything they would enjoy doing which would bring in money should the need arise. Even if they never have to support the family single-handed, such interests outside the home will help to keep the marriage fresh and alive.

A SPECIAL RELATIONSHIP

Christians believe that their relationship with God through Jesus Christ is what gives them strength in their everyday lives and security for the future. This does not mean that they are unaffected by the sorrows of suffering, death and bereavement, but that they have God's help and comfort to draw on when tragedy strikes, and hope for a life beyond death shared with God himself.

The reality of Jesus' promise, often used in the words of the funeral service, can be proved by everyone who trusts themselves to God's care: 'I am the resurrection and the life. Whoever believes in me will live, even though he dies; and whoever lives and believes in me will never die.'